"Most great music is considered bad in some respect or other when it first appears. The reason is simple: greatness involves newness, and the new is 'bad' inasmuch as it does not conform to the familiar or customary. You have to get used to things, especially things which hit you."

Hans Keller

Also by Robert Matthew-Walker

Muhammad Ali – His Fights in the Ring
Rachmaninoff – His Life and Times
Edvard Grieg – A Biographical Study
The Recordings of Edvard Grieg
Alun Hoddinott on Record
New World Music – Aspects of New Age
Elvis Presley – A Study in Music
Heartbreak Hotel – The Life and Music of Elvis Presley
Simon and Garfunkel
David Bowie – Theatre of Music
Madonna – The Biography
The Art of Sir Eugène Goossens (*in preparation*)
Liszt's Pupils Recorded – A Biographical Discography (*in preparation*)
The Keller Column – Essays by Hans Keller (*editor*)
The Symphonies of Robert Simpson (*editor*)
Cincinnati Interludes – Essays by Sir Eugène Goossens (*editor*)

Havergal Brian
Reminiscences and Observations

Robert Matthew-Walker

DGR Books
St Austell

First published in 1995 by
DGR Books
Kenwyn
Greensplat
St. Austell, Cornwall PL26 8XX
England

© Copyright Robert Matthew-Walker 1995

All rights reserved

Typeset by
Able Graphics,
St. Austell, Cornwall

Printed by
Hartnolls,
Victoria Square, Bodmin, Cornwall

ISBN 1 898343 04 7

Contents

	Page
Preface	7
I – Background	13
II – First Meetings	33
III – The 'Gothic' Performed	45
IV – Further Contact	57
V – A Passing Tribute	65
VI – Later Plans	77
VII – A Redeemed Artist	87
Appendix I – The Havergal Brian Society	112
Appendix II – Performances of the 'Gothic' Symphony	114
Appendix III – Released Recordings of the 'Gothic' Symphony	117
Index	119

Illustrations:

From a photograph of Havergal Brian
by Douglas Glass, August 1960 .... Cover
Drawing of Havergal Brian by F. Furnivall
(reproduced by permission of the artist) .... Frontispiece
Facsimile of Havergal Brian: the opening
of the Tenth Symphony (1954), in the
composer's manuscript (reproduced by
permission of United Music Publishers Ltd.) .... Page 52

Preface

This book has come into being through the persistence of one young man and the insight of another. Some years ago, I mentioned to Mark Doran that I had known Havergal Brian, had corresponded with and visited him in the late 1950s and early 1960s. Mark, a member of the Havergal Brian Society, was very interested to learn of this association, and urged me to set down my recollections of Brian. It had happened a long time ago and I felt I needed time to collect my thoughts and whatever material I still had. Mark was quite persistent and would often remind me to write down what I knew of Havergal Brian or consent to a series of interviews.

It was a flattering suggestion and although I considered it from time to time, other, more pressing, matters conspired to prevent me from giving much attention to the idea. But his prompting nagged at me; as the years have passed I have become more convinced than ever that Brian is a great composer and, as such, the recollections of anyone who knew him should be set down.

By chance, in the summer of 1994 I received a leaflet advertising a concert to be given on August 5th in the Duke's Hall of London's Royal Academy of Music by a new professional orchestra. This was the London Orchestra of Saint Cecilia, conducted by James Kelleher, the programme of which included the first public performance of Havergal Brian's Symphony No 16.

I could hardly not go. As a young man, on leave from the British Army, I had visited Havergal Brian at his home within days of him completing this very symphony, when he had been keen to show me certain passages in it. Now, 34 years later, this same work was to be heard for the first time in public.

I knew it was a masterpiece; a good recording of it, made by the London Philharmonic under Myer Fredman, was issued in 1975, but was long since out of print. For many years I had baulked at what seemed to me to be a never-ending series of largely amateur public performances of works by Brian, demanding works that cried out for experienced professionals: was this to be another such occasion?

I need not have worried. The concert began with a masterly account of the Brahms Violin Concerto by Krysia Osostowicz – both soloist and conductor were impressive: during the interval I spoke with the critic Geoffrey Crankshaw and mentioned to him my friendship with Brian. "You should write your autobiography, Bob," he said, "you've met so many great musicians." I told him I had no intention of doing that, but the idea of writing down my memories of Havergal Brian received another impetus from Geoffrey. If I harboured doubts as to Kelleher's ability to grasp and project Brian's Sixteenth Symphony, in the event I was astonished. His was undoubtedly a reading of penetration and insight; of course, the orchestral playing could have been improved upon, but this was a real performance of some stature. I was also intrigued to see Brian's remarks to me concerning the symphony quoted in the programme note, but it was the nature of James Kelleher's performance that made a deep impression.

This great work had been finally revealed as such in public and

Preface

this young conductor deserved much credit.

After the concert, I spoke with James Kelleher and thanked him for what he had done for my old friend. It was this performance, and what Geoffrey Crankshaw had said, that vividly brought back my association with the composer after all these years. I soon came to the conclusion that Mark Doran had been right all along: I had been privileged to know a great composer and I had a duty to put down on record all that I knew about him at first hand and of the events with which I was connected regarding some of the early recordings and plans concerning Brian's works which had never before been made public.

It is the nature of such recollections that they tend to be somewhat autobiographical and I was not sure that my association amounted to very much; there are others whose association with Brian was greater than mine. My publisher, Geoffrey Lee Cooper, learned of these reminiscences and asked if they might make a book. It so happened that I was able to tell him that he appeared in the narrative himself, for I have known him since we were both members of the same Music Club in the 1950s, which indirectly led to my meeting Havergal Brian in the first place.

British musical life in the 1990s is very different from what it was 40 or 50 years ago, and I have quoted from several items of contemporary writing about Brian by two outstanding musicians, both of whom I later got to know quite well: Harold Truscott and Robert Simpson, which so fired my enthusiasm in those days. It is Robert Simpson's name that appears more frequently in this book, for it was as a result of meeting him through the Music Club in 1958 that I got to know Havergal Brian personally, and Simpson's efforts on Brian's behalf are now well-known. I did not meet Harold

Truscott until much later and got to know him very well in the late 1970s, when I planned and produced the first recording, with Harold present, of any of his music – three of his piano sonatas, Nos 9, 13 and 15 played by Peter Jacobs – a record which was released on the Altarus label. Harold and I spoke often of Havergal Brian, whom Harold had known well. He told me of curious events Brian recounted to him, one being that Brian would tie up the manuscript of his 'Gothic' Symphony at night before going to bed, and in the morning would find it opened, the pages mixed up. This did not wholly surprise me; at times, I found Brian a strange man in ways I find difficult to describe – there was occasionally an 'air' about him – although the night-time events seemed to me to be nothing more than the results of sleep-walking.

This book also contains previously unpublished correspondence between Sir Eugène Goossens and Havergal Brian. Goossens was one of several major conductors who tried, without success, to mount Brian's legendary 'Gothic' Symphony in the 1930s, but were thwarted by the cost involved. Sir Eugène was able to attend the eventual 'Gothic' world premiere in London in 1961.

For permission to quote from copyright material, I must thank Robert Simpson and Mrs Harold Truscott; I must also thank Mrs Jean Furnivall for permission to quote from letters written by her father, Havergal Brian, and Miss Pamela Main for permission to publish the letters of Sir Eugène Goossens.

Further thanks are due also to Mark Doran, Geoffrey Lee Cooper, Denby Richards of *Musical Opinion*, Christopher Breunig of *Hi Fi News and Record Review*, Nigel Lea-Jones, Edward Johnson, Malcolm Smith, Malcolm MacDonald and Alan Marshall.

It has been a pleasant experience to recount these memories,

Preface

yet I feel the climate for a proper acceptance of Havergal Brian's music has still not yet arrived; many an opportunity for performance of his work has not been taken by those in a position to advance his cause – and today's audiences should hear his symphonies and operas not because Havergal Brian is a 'cause', but because his art speaks with a greater relevance to society today than the works of few comparable twentieth-century masters. My definition of a great composer is one whose music one finds one cannot live without and over the years I have found myself returning again and again to Brian's amazing series of symphonies.

I trust I have been able in these pages to convey some of the initial excitement and power with which Brian's music hit me as a young man. It still has that strength, which I find has grown with time, so that the young conductor James Kelleher's splendid reading of Brian's Sixteenth Symphony in August 1994 was hardly less revelatory to me than those early pioneering performances I heard all those years ago. Brian's time is still to come, and we must envy those future generations who will know his music so much better than we do now. If James Kelleher is anything to go by, that time is closer now and seems more secure than for some summers past. But the public cannot, of course, express an opinion on music with which it is never given the chance of coming into contact, and whereas in the past fifty years or so we have witnessed the general establishment within the international repertoire of the importance of music that was previously ignored or simply unknown – virtually all of Vivaldi's output, the compositions of Bruckner, Mahler, Rachmaninoff and Nielsen, much of the work of the Second Viennese School: these are the more notable examples of music which, when I was a boy, was rarely heard in Britain. In each

HAVERGAL BRIAN

case there was a dedicated band of supporters who kept faith with these composers, who lobbied for performances, for radio broadcasts and recordings and whose efforts paid off in the end, to the benefit of all. In the case of Havergal Brian, we still have a fair way to go, but James Kelleher's performance of the Sixteenth Symphony could not have come about were it not for the efforts of the Havergal Brian Society. This thriving and effective voice in the dissemination of the composer's music was founded in 1974 and has done a very great deal in locating missing material of the composer, notably the original full score of his opera 'The Tigers', lost for thirty years, in subventing performances and recordings, and in the regular publication of information and news on the composer and his work together with the publication of his music. Details of the Havergal Brian Society will be found on pages 112-113.

Robert Matthew-Walker,
London, February 1995

Chapter I
Background

My introduction to Havergal Brian came about through the composer, Robert Simpson, whom I had first met in 1957 when he consented to become President of the Eltham Music Club, of which I was a member. I believe that Simpson had been present at the National Federation of Gramophone Societies' Hoddesdon Conference that year where he had met two officers of the Club, Derek Payne and Peter Laming, and these gentlemen had extended the invitation to him. I was surprised that he bothered to accept, frankly, for we were only a small music society that met in a room above a pub in south-east London, whereas at that time Simpson lived in North London, in Muswell Hill, and, as at that time he did not possess a car, his journey home had to be made by public transport. As the Club meetings did not end until 10.30pm, the pub's 'closing time' under existing legislation, and last goodbyes were not said until some time after that, his journey home by public transport – bus, train or tube – meant that he would not arrive at his house until quite late. He did not, of course, come to every meeting – perhaps two or three times a year – but it was a kind and friendly gesture which was much appreciated by the members and which had long-term implications for me.

The HMV record of Simpson's First Symphony under Boult

had just been issued, and, by way of 'introducing' him to the Club, it was played at a meeting prior to his first visit. I was deeply impressed by the work – it made an immediate impact upon me which has never waned. Edmund Rubbra – whom I was later also to get to know quite well – wrote in flattering terms of the Symphony in the EMG 'Monthly Letter', a piece reprinted in a book on Simpson's Symphonies I edited in 1990, and Hugh Ottoway had also just written an article on the Symphony in the 'Musical Times'. Having read what Rubbra had written, I obtained the disc, the study score published by Alfred Lengnick and Ottoway's piece and got to know the work intimately. When Simpson came to talk to us, I was keen to tell him of my enthusiasm for his Symphony; although he responded to my eagerness, much of what he had to say on this first visit, to me and to the Club's members in general, was about the composer Havergal Brian.

For many people, in those days Brian was not even a name; I had only heard one work of Brian's, the Eighth Symphony, in one of what I now know were two broadcast performances which had been given by the London Philharmonic Orchestra under Sir Adrian Boult in 1954 on the BBC Third Programme, the precursor of Radio 3. When I say 'heard', one must remember that in those days FM broadcasting did not exist, and, even if it had, the finances of a working-class family could not have run to acquiring an FM tuner for their 14-year-old son. Reception of the Third Programme on our old radio was often bedevilled by interference; and I do not think I heard Brian's Eighth either properly, or even all the way through, in 1954. However, one overriding memory of the work remains vivid after 40 years: the extraordinary, even frightening, opening which gripped my impressionable imagination and, now

Background

I think about it, may have spurred my determination to become a composer myself. I learned, much later, that another work of Brian's, his *Dr Merryheart* Overture – a kind of English *Till Eulenspiegel* – had been broadcast on December 27th, 1956, but I had not heard this.

Simpson was keen to bring to our attention the forthcoming broadcast by the BBC of Brian's Ninth Symphony, and spoke at some length of Brian and his neglect. It was an extraordinary story, of course, and it seemed to all of us then that if anyone was in a position to help Brian it was Simpson through his post at the BBC. I had known something of Brian in other ways; I had long been in the habit of spending every Saturday in London, since I was about 12, and spending all my money on records (both 78rpm and LPs), scores, books and manuscript paper in the music shops and second-hand stores in the West End and Soho. Nothing else mattered to me, and in this way I had bought second-hand copies of two books by Reginald Nettel, *Music in the Five Towns* and *Ordeal by Music – The Strange Experience of Havergal Brian*, both of which, especially the latter of course, were concerned with Brian. The latter seems to me to be one of the most astounding books on music to have been published in the middle of this century – would such a thing, a study of a composer whose music was unplayed and unpublished and remained utterly ignored, ever be issued today by an established publishing house? I also bought copies of a few works by Brian which were still in print: the Prelude and Fugue in C minor and a Double Fugue in E flat major, both for solo piano, and I had come across some old part-songs dating from about 1912. Some years before 1957 I had damaged my left shoulder whilst working as a warehouse boy and the result was gradually to cause

HAVERGAL BRIAN

me to lose the flexibility of my left hand in playing the piano; it was indeed a bitter realisation for me that my piano technique would never again achieve its previous fluency, and works that I longed to play – and could, at one time – were now beyond me, apart from private study at home. One of these pieces was Brian's C minor Prelude and Fugue but I could not play it properly now. Thanks to a gifted osteopath whom I had consulted for a trapped sciatic nerve and who asked me why I never mentioned the trouble with my left shoulder, I discovered, many years later, that my shoulder accident resulted in a twisted deep muscular lesion – she could tell, just by looking at it. My accident had forced me to examine works from a more analytical standpoint, and I concluded that the piano pieces by Brian were unlike anything else I had seen by an English composer.

When I was about 10 years old I had acquired some early issues of the magazine *Music Survey*, though I hardly understood them! But I knew I had to have them, even then; I was attracted by the 'feel' of what they conveyed. Here were writers who did not seem to get much of a hearing elsewhere, and the composers about whom they wrote interested me, even at that young age, and furthermore these composers were, in the main, ignored by other publications and newspapers. The point is that the two opening sentences of a review in one issue of *Music Survey* hit me with uncomprehending astonishment; it was by Harold Truscott, reviewing these same two piano pieces by Brian.

This is what he wrote:

"That Havergal Brian is one of the major composers this country has so far produced, I have no doubt. When the public at

Background

large will have a chance to find out for itself it is impossible to say. I do not agree with the critic who, when reviewing Nettel's book *Ordeal by Music*, said that Brian had had his chance – in other words, it had come and gone and now it is too late. For whatever reason, he has not had it. The story of the constant string of misfortunes which has attended as baulked a career as can be found in musical history can be read fully in the book mentioned above. The same critic implied that, the day of large orchestras having gone by (has it?) along with the Romantic era, Brian was a back number. It would be interesting to know what works and performances of Brian the reviewer had heard.

The passing of the large orchestra is an illusion. All that has passed is a reason for using it. English scoring, as a rule, is not a strong point, and composers like Vaughan Williams, Britten, Walton, Rawsthorne, etc., are now using large orchestras for the mere production of noise, and employing unnecessary doublings which make a Schumann symphony, always the subject of much ado about nothing in this respect, a model of good scoring by comparison. They have completely failed to understand the good sense of composers such as Bruckner and Mahler – the latter especially understanding fully that, in order to produce the chamber effect which is his aim in all the major symphonies, it is necessary to use a very large orchestra, not to double or quadruple every part and so produce a noisy blur, but to have as many strands clearly audible as possible. There is not a note in these scores which cannot be clearly heard in even a bad performance; I defy anyone to say the same for the Vaughan Williams 4th, 5th or 6th [Symphonies], or Britten's *Sinfonia da Requiem* or Walton's Symphony, or Rawsthorne's *Symphonic Studies* or Violin Concerto [no 1].

This Brian clearly understands also, and, in the scores I know at all well, the *Dr Merryheart* Overture, the *Fantastic Variations on an Old Rhyme* and the 'Gothic' Symphony, he shows a mastery which is rare in that every instrument is necessary and contributes its quota to a texture clear in every detail.

As to the music, everyone must find that for himself. I know its importance for me, but I shall not presume to dictate to others. What is necessary, before Brian can be either accepted or dismissed with fairness by the musical public in general, is an adequate number of performances of his major works. That the music is Romantic is true, but it is true in a way that musicians today misunderstand. Part of the reason for this misunderstanding lies in the problem of large orchestras and in the size of the works concerned. Almost the only thing which today governs the length of a work for a listener, musician, critic or otherwise, is the clock. What makes such works as the symphonies of Bruckner and Mahler, and I will say Brian, independent of this mechanical device is their magnificent sense of proportion – one of the prime reasons for the size of the orchestra used. And, in Bruckner and Mahler's case, the origin of this proportion lies in a great achievement of Schubert which is obscure today, merely because proportion has disappeared from our scheme of things. Until this is seen, composers will continue to produce short works for large orchestras which actually sound much longer and ten times more tedious than any Bruckner or Mahler symphony, because there is no proportion, and therefore no sense.

Brian has this sense of proportion: in fact, whether it is there consciously or unconsciously, there is evident to me, in such work

Background

of his as I know, a definite Schubertian ancestry (I speak of structure and of nothing else) which reduces his enormous creations to normal size – that is, the right size for our ears.

At the moment, his larger works must wait for their appreciation, which will inevitably come, until some return to a sense of lasting values and proportion has been effected, although, in the process of delay, we may lacerate a man's soul. That is the old, the human way of thanks, and Brian, no doubt, has by now learned it to the full. In the meantime, we may well occupy our time in getting acquainted with such of his smaller works as are available, and be grateful to Messrs. Augener's for thus belatedly publishing these two works for piano. (They were composed in 1924!) They are both fine examples of his mature way of thinking, in a texture which owes more than a little to Reger, although only in a few instances does the sound approximate to the German master. The Prelude and Fugue are fine to play and easy to read, with a mastery in distribution of effect which is content not to anticipate climaxes and shows a view of the piano as essentially pianistic as his orchestral thinking is essentially orchestral.

The Double Fugue is a huge structure which might well take its place beside the great series by Reger. Its effect is as immediate on the hearer as in the Reger fugues, but its layout is marred by one fault. No doubt with the intention of making it easy to read, Brian has in many places laid out the four parts on four staves. In practice, this makes superhuman demands on the reader, and it is a pity that such a magnificent work should be placed at such a disadvantage, one which can easily be put right. It is to be hoped that in a future edition this will be done."

This was Harold Truscott, writing about a major composer about whom it seemed few people knew anything in 1949, and you may readily imagine that it was Truscott's words, more than anything else, that impelled me to try to hear Brian's Eighth Symphony in 1954. Today as an adult I understand the review, and might be critical of certain aspects of the points he makes, but it had done its job so far as I was concerned: Brian's music clearly meant something important to Harold Truscott in 1949, and if it meant something important to him, it might mean something important to others also, including me.

Therefore, by about 1957, after having assimilated a fair amount of information on him, I was reasonably aware of Brian, and with Simpson's encouragement I looked forward to the broadcast of Brian's Ninth Symphony early in 1958. Quite frankly, I was astounded by it; it would be quite wrong to say I 'understood' the work, but I knew then that it was a challenge – especially the concluding pages, which had me falling off the little wicker chair in my room in my excitement. I had, by this time, bought a better radio of my own out of my wages from a part-time job I now had in a soft-drinks factory. I was then 'stuck', as the saying goes, in my own Second Symphony, and hearing Brian's Ninth spurred me to finish it; I think the ferocious ending of my Symphony may owe a little to that of Brian's Ninth, although the idiom is somewhat different!

When Simpson was ill for some weeks I wrote to him on behalf of the Club and he invited me to visit him. I would visit the Simpsons' Muswell Hill home three or four times a year, and on one visit he asked me if I was a composer: I had hardly dare mention my own music to him, but one evening at the Music Club we had

Background

had a festive evening, during which a tape was played of a 'musical party' I had improvised at a friend's house, which sent up various figures and composers, including Britten, some of whose folk-song settings I felt were unbelievably arch. I had improvised a setting of *Inside the Castle Walls*, singing as Pears and accompanying myself at the piano. It was all D major, flattened sevenths in the vocal line and so on, but I have to say it brought the house down. When I next visited Simpson, he said that only a composer could have taken Britten off so wickedly and asked to see my work. I had not finished the Second Symphony, and was most diffident about him examining my music: the point was, I had come to find out about him, not the other way about, and I put off the fateful day until I felt I had something worth showing him. In the end, I never did show the Symphony to him – when it was finished, I felt some things happened in it with which he would not concur, and I admired him so much I did not want to risk his possible consternation. Perhaps I need not have worried; I did show it to Edmund Rubbra, twenty years later, and he said to let him know when it was to be performed, as he would like to be there.

In 1958 the publishers Anthony Blond brought out a *Guide to Modern Music on Records*, edited by Robert Simpson and Oliver Prenn. To this interesting and valuable book, which had a Foreword by Edmund Rubbra, Simpson had contributed an Introduction, which, as much for its common sense as for the various points he made, had a big influence on my thinking. Characteristically, he ended his Introduction with a plea. Calling for attention to be paid to "one particular genius, not because he is more important than anyone else, but because he has hitherto been outrageously neglected, not only by the gramophone companies, but by the whole musical world", Simpson went on, "Havergal Brian is now in his eighty-second year; his case is an extraordinary one, almost without parallel. He reached his late seventies before he was allowed to hear any of his symphonies (he has now composed twelve) and has thus far heard only three. For many years it has been customary, if his name has been mentioned at all, to dismiss him as one of those composers who became bogged down in heavily derivative, extravagant post-Romanticism in the early part of the century (it will be noticed that Hugh Ottoway, through lack of opportunity to know Brian's late works, has not unnaturally fallen to this conclusion [a chapter in the book, *Twentieth-Century English Music*, by Ottoway shows less than true understanding of several composers]). Recent performances of Brian's Eighth and Ninth Symphonies on the BBC Third Programme, however, have revealed an altogether different composer. Through decade after decade of complete neglect, this iron-willed musician has composed steadily one massive work after another, apparently without hope of ever hearing any of them and without making more than token attempts to interest concert-giving organizations in them. He has achieved pure detachment from personal ambition, so far as his reputation is concerned, but his music has developed with astonishing power and consistency in accordance with a deeper ambition to find and conquer all that lies in the depths of his mind. There is, perhaps, something almost awesome in the thought of a man composing steadfastly in obscurity, certain of his own goal and heedless of outward success, and one's sympathies might easily lead one to an over-valuation of his music. But such music as Brian's does not encourage shallow sympathy; its strangeness and granite-like strength reflect with complete faithfulness and profound imagina-

Background

tion a mind of immense character that needs no pity. The Ninth Symphony is one of the greatest and most concentrated of English works; its brooding first movement grapples with the deep problems discovered by a spirit that has been driven inwards upon itself, compelled to penetrate into mine beneath dark, hidden mine in its own being, and the unshakeable grandeur at the end of the symphony is a thing far more powerful than ordinary triumph – it is like some titanic rock that has resisted the slow erosion of millennia. The music of this and his other late symphonies is never predictable; nor is it in any sense 'old-fashioned'. Its course is always entirely unforeseeable and entirely inevitable. It does not cultivate harmonic harshness as a norm, yet it contains many strange and wonderful sounds, such as could have been created in no time but the present. Brian's powers of organic construction, too, are remarkable in a period when many composers, having witnessed the apparent destruction of a whole way of musical thought, can do no better than play like naive children with jig-saw puzzles made from what they imagine to be fragments of the wreck. The strength of Brian lies in the foundations of his art; nothing is calculated for 'effect' (he has nothing to do with what Sir Hugh Casson has so aptly called 'look-no-hands architecture') yet the real effect is utterly unlike that of any other music. This great old man is still exploring and finding new things; few composers may be said to have done this after the age of seventy. We younger composers who have benefited so greatly from the help of the British Council, the B.B.C., and other bodies, should be ashamed to accept it until this octogenarian, the master of us all, has received his due."

This was powerful and exciting stuff for me – and for other people as well. In mid-1958 Simpson told me of the BBC's plans to premiere Brian's Tenth Symphony, and would I like to attend. Would I?! Six or eight members of the Music Club went in a party. Amongst them was Geoffrey Lee Cooper, now publisher of this book, and the late Don Mather, and I believe Peter Laming was also present. It was an unforgettable occasion: it was a live broadcast and began late – after 9pm. In the first half Hans Werner Henze conducted the British premiere of his Sonata for Strings followed by a beautiful performance of Mozart's Piano Concerto K 503 by Artur Balsam, conducted by Stanley Pope – a superb conductor who was briefly signed to Philips Records in London by the late Douglas Pudney and made two records with the Royal Philharmonic Orchestra: the world premiere recording of Schumann's Fourth Symphony in the original orchestration, and four of Elgar's *Pomp and Circumstance* marches. I was to meet Stanley Pope soon after in Robert Simpson's office at the BBC. A pity this excellent conductor was not more used by record companies. The second half, which was devoted to the premiere of Brian's Tenth Symphony, began after 10pm, and during the interval I was astonished to see many notable people there. It may be that some were attracted by Henze, then only 32 and already established as a world figure. Sir Eugène Goossens, one of my boyhood heroes – whom I felt instinctively had been set up for the unsavoury pornography case in which he had recently been caught; many years later, I learned that my instincts then were correct – was at the studios also, and I, with some temerity, introduced myself to him, saying how much I admired his work as a conductor and composer, and that I had many of his records. He was very kind and gracious; it was Eugène Goossens III, as conductor of the Cincinnati Symphony Orchestra from 1931 to 1947, who tried valiantly to mount the

Background

premiere of Brian's 'Gothic' Symphony in the USA after Brian had written a revealing letter to him soon after Goossens had taken up his appointment in Ohio. The references to cathedrals are significant.

"1931

Sept. 28

1, Jasper Road,
Upper Norwood
London, S.E.19.

My dear Eugène,

In your busy life you may have forgotten that when you were being knocked about a little too much I wrote to you from Marine Square Brighton and begged of you to take courage. I said that you must think of the vast network of cathedrals which stretched across Europe from St Sophia (Constantinople) to Durham, for all were built under the most awful odds and difficulties. Apparently that was not the end of it for you have built a cathedral in America.

I also built one and it is called the Gothic Symphony. It lasts a whole evening. First three parts are instrumental only, conceived in a big sweep on majestic lines for large orchestra – woodwind in fours – bass flute, bass oboe, basset horn, 4 Tpts, 6 Hrns, 4 Trbs, 2 Tubas.

The Finale, a setting of the "Te Deum Laudamus", is for an 8-part chorus and orchestra principals. The 8-part chorus is a unit, but it often spreads to four four-part independent choirs, often kept apart for antiphonal purposes and then drawn together and massed. The setting occupies 2 hours, it embraces every ancient and modern form of choral technique.

The orchestra is enormous. I have all the w.wind in complete families, even the Pedal Clarinet is there. In the Judex crederis treated as the central movement of the setting, which is in three parts, I have four independent brass and tympani orchestras. Just before the final Non confundar which ends by the way in voices only in closest low harmonies, I have a final cataclysm from all the Brass and the Tympani. If this kind of mammoth handling appeals to you, please get in touch with Cranz & Co who have taken over this work for publication, but in January 1933. As you may realise from the works I have written and having to earn my living in addition, I have had no time to see anyone. But I think often about you, often read about you and when I get an opportunity I write about you. It is one of my few pleasures to think of you my dear Eugène.

> Always your friend,
> Havergal Brian.

I got knocked about after you left for America.

Lost my home entirely, but I stuck to my Symphony and Opera."

Brian had not written to Eugène Goossens entirely out of the blue; he had heard operas conducted by Goossens's grandfather, Eugène Goossens I, and by Eugène II, and Brian as a musical journalist had written about Goossens – arguably the most brilliantly-gifted of all British musicians of his generation – in the 1920s; they had met on several occasions, and Eugène Goossens himself had plans to conduct Brian's music before 1931.

Goossens took up Brian's suggestion and obtained a score of the 'Gothic' from Cranz. But January 1933 was the month in which Hitler's National Socialist Party had been elected in Germany, and the history of Europe had embarked upon a frightening course.

Background

Having, at long last, found a publisher, the irony for Brian was that things associated with Germany were increasingly regarded with some distaste. He was again the Outsider.

Eugène Goossens's keenness to give the 'Gothic' in the USA was eventually thwarted by the huge cost involved when America was still in the throes of the Depression. Goossens's plans were particularly sound: the Queen City of Cincinnati has held the biggest biannual choral festival in the United States for well over 100 years. The voices were there, and we know from his outstanding series of recordings that the Orchestra was of international stature. It is a tragedy that Goossens's plans never came to fruition.

The premiere of Brian's Tenth Symphony took place, as I write, 36 years ago; the memory is as vivid as if it were yesterday. I could not believe the orchestra Brian had asked for: the wind and thunder machines made an amazing sight and before I had heard a note of the work I eagerly anticipated it. From the first bars of the Symphony, I was enthralled. As it unfolded I knew I was present at the first performance of great music, a rare experience hardly ever encountered today. If Brian's Ninth Symphony had impressed me, his Tenth knocked me sideways; the deep moment of 'stillness' and the astounding 'storm' that follows it seemed to me to be passages of great inspiration and technical execution and do so still. I could not believe what I was hearing and from then on I had no doubt that Brian was a great composer. At the end of the Symphony, Brian – wearing a rusty-coloured tweed suit – came forward, his right arm raised, to congratulate and thank Stanley Pope and the Philharmonia, quite a few of whose members stayed (at that late hour) to applaud him and to talk with him afterwards. One must remember that the Philharmonia of the 1950s was without question the finest orchestra in the country by far at that time – this had to have been the finest first performance of any of Brian's works up to then, and arguably since.

Excited by what I had heard, but too overwhelmed to go up and talk to Brian himself then, I returned home in an elated mood. I could hardly sleep; and I penned a letter to Brian, expressing my enthusiasm. I did not know where he lived so I looked in the London phone book. There was an address in Northwood, Middlesex and I posted the letter on a Sunday, probably November 9th, to catch the 4.15 afternoon collection. Imagine my surprise when I received a reply on the Tuesday, two days later, not from Northwood but from 1, The Marlinespike, Shoreham-by-Sea in Sussex. As an example of Post Office speed this was uncanny but Harold Truscott told me that there were odd things about Brian and correspondence.

His letter thanked me for writing to him, and for my comments on the Tenth Symphony; he praised Robert Simpson for being the prime mover of the broadcast and asked me to get in touch, if I wished, with Miss Eve Barsham, who had copies of his recent scores and whose address he gave.

A few weeks later, on December 20th 1958, I was again at the BBC's Maida Vale studios, to hear Brian's Eighth Symphony. This was given by the BBC Symphony Orchestra under its then relatively new chief conductor, Rudolf Schwarz. I was there not through an invitation from Simpson, but through Arthur Leavins, who had for some years in the 1950s been leader of the Royal Philharmonic Orchestra under Sir Thomas Beecham and who had joined the BBC Symphony Orchestra a year or so earlier to sit alongside Paul Beard on the first desk. I had been taking some rather

Background

desultory piano lessons from Arthur Leavins's wife, the pianist Mary Baddeley, for a few years – these lessons were desultory not owing to any shortcomings on her part, but because of my inability to overcome the problems of finger dexterity in my left hand, following my injury. Through her husband, I was able to attend many BBC Symphony Orchestra broadcasts, and I also became a fairly frequent visitor to their home in Bromley. I was very grateful to them for their kindnesses to me, and when Arthur Leavins asked me if I would like to attend the rehearsals and broadcast of Brian's Eighth he was surprised when I told him I had heard (at least part of) the 1954 Boult premiere, and had actually just written to Brian, having been at the premiere of the Tenth; Leavins was unaware that the Eighth Symphony had been done before.

I remember little of Schwarz's performance of No 8, other than I did not think it was in quite the same class as Pope and the Philharmonia in the Tenth. I cannot remember what else was in the programme, but I do remember being in something of a cleft stick with regard to my reaction. The opening of the Eighth under Schwarz was as frightening as ever; but I knew from Arthur Leavins that Beard, in particular, had been rather bolshy about the Symphony in rehearsal – something which I witnessed myself – and I do not think that, because of this, the orchestra played with quite the required committedness that the score demanded, as some had taken their cue from Beard. I do not think Arthur Leavins shared my keenness for Brian's music, either, and there may well have been an element within the orchestra that rebelled against what was already then in some quarters perceived to be a case of 'special pleading': it was the first time the BBC's own Symphony Orchestra had played a work by Brian for many years. In the event it was not at

HAVERGAL BRIAN

all a bad performance, but if I say I can still recall details of Pope's account of No 10, but remember little of Schwarz in No 8, I think the point is made. I am not sure if Brian himself was present, either; it may well have been that he was, but I do not recall seeing him on that occasion.

However, I wrote to Brian telling him of hearing his Eighth Symphony properly at last, and we exchanged several further letters during 1959, after Robert Simpson had visited the Music Club to give a fascinating talk devoted entirely to Brian, playing tapes of the Eighth and Ninth Symphonies, and bringing scores for us to follow. Amongst the most avid score-readers in the Club was Ray Burford, who at that time had a very successful career as sales director for a food company. The BBC had programmed the Ninth again, with Norman Del Mar conducting, in February 1959 but I was unable to hear that broadcast as I had to work late at the soft-drinks factory.

The climax of the year, for me and for the growing number of Brian enthusiasts at that time, was the Third Programme concert on Thursday, November 5th by the London Symphony Orchestra under Harry Newstone in which Brian's Eleventh and Twelfth Symphonies were first heard, together with the *Dr Merryheart* Overture. I had been impatiently looking forward to hearing this, but the deaths in a car crash the previous Friday of two young friends who worked in the factory with me and both of whose funerals were held on that same Thursday, meant that I missed the broadcast. I wrote to Brian, expressing my disappointment and he wrote a long sympathetic letter back telling me of a friend of his who had been killed on a motorcycle before the War; his letter included some details on the Eleventh Symphony, with music examples, and

Background

he expressed the wish that I might be able to hear tapes of the symphonies, which Robert Simpson might be good enough to organise for me. I am glad to say that that is indeed what happened, and Simpson told me that when the performances were over he sat with Brian in the pub later, Brian with a glass of Guinness. "D'you know," Brian said to Simpson, "this is the greatest day of my life." But more, and greater, things were to come. The Eleventh Symphony seemed to me to be a new Brian; the opening paragraph for strings in the first movement has a spaciousness as if inhabiting a similar mood to that which begins Sibelius's Sixth Symphony and although the beginning of the second movement has been compared with the opening of Mahler's Fourth Symphony, by Malcolm MacDonald amongst others, it has always seemed to me to be more akin to a modern version of the second movement of Beethoven's Eighth Symphony. The two symphonies confirmed my enthusiasm for Brian's work: I think the Twelfth is perhaps the best introduction to his later music for the newcomer.

A few weeks later I knew that I would be joining the Army, and around this time I learned that I would soon be in that part of Sussex where Brian lived. On the spur of the moment, I telephoned to ask if I might call. Mrs Brian answered the phone, and told me that her husband was in the bath. When I told her that I would be near Shoreham on Monday, February 1st, she asked if I would like to visit them and stay to lunch.

I accepted with alacrity. The next day, I received a letter from Brian, the tone being rather stiff – "I understand you will be coming to lunch" – and it occurred to me I should use the opportunity of my visit to record an interview with him, if possible. I wrote to Robert Simpson, telling him of my impending visit and idea to record an interview; he replied that "It would be good to get something down on tape." I bought a small portable recorder for that purpose, of the kind some reporters used in those days, and took it with me. My father advanced me the money – £25 – for the machine.

Chapter II
First Meetings

February 1st, 1960 was a bright, coolish day in southern England, with a momentary touch of warmth to herald the coming spring as I walked from the station to the modern new bungalow, not far from the beach on the outskirts of Shoreham, where the Brians lived. Mrs Brian opened the door, and immediately Havergal came along the passageway to the left to introduce himself. He was about five feet four, thick-set, and gave the impression that in earlier days he might have been a boxer or at least have taken regular hard exercise. He certainly did not look 84 years old – perhaps 60 or so – and was dressed in a dark suit with a contrasting waistcoat. He wore a bow-tie, which certainly suited him. Our first few moments were a little stiff. As Mrs Brian busied herself in the kitchen, we sat and talked, somewhat uneasily on my part, I have to say, for I got the impression that my presence was something he would rather have not had to contend with, but was obliged to because of Mrs Brian's invitation, or that he had other, more pressing, things on his mind.

Gradually, the conversation began to flow and, within a short while, Mrs Brian called us to the table. It was roast mutton, served with walnuts. Brian had a beer, and so did I, and this seemed to do the trick, for his conversation now became more relaxed and at ease – but only in comparison, for he did not talk very much at any one time. Mrs Brian asked after my family, and told me quite firmly that whatever happened I was never to get married if I wanted to become a composer! I remember Brian being somewhat miffed by this remark, a kind of muffled "hrrumph!", but it was not pursued. We spoke a lot about music, and Brian seemed genuinely interested when he learned that I also composed but I did not tell him of what I had written. We talked especially about Robert Simpson, for whom Brian had the highest regard, and Brian was also keen to learn of the Music Club. I told him that I had visited Simpson at the end of December, on the 31st to be exact, when he had shown me the first pages of his Third Symphony, which he had begun on the 28th of that month. If it was Simpson's intention at that early stage of composition to dedicate the finished Symphony to Brian, he did not tell me – or if he did, I did not mention it to Brian.

I think that the dedication of Brian's Thirteenth Symphony to Simpson, completed in the early part of December 1959, may have been the spur for Simpson to begin his own Third Symphony: these events were within a few days of each other and another Brian connexion between both symphonies is a purely musical one. Simpson's Third Symphony, which was completed in 1962, is concerned at one level with the establishing of C major out of, or alongside, its adjacent B flat major. Brian's 'Gothic' symphony traverses a tonal route that proceeds inevitably from D major to E major. The 'adjacent tonality' scheme is, of course, very different in both works, but I should not be surprised to learn that, as an initial idea, the challenge of writing a work in which a tonality is estab-lished through its relationship with its neighbour – which informs the 'Gothic' – was unconsciously suggested to Simpson by study-ing the score of Brian's gigantic symphony.

First Meetings

At this first meeting I told Brian of my surprise that he had reached his Thirteenth Symphony, but I was amazed when he told me that some days before he had completed Symphony No 14 and he was making a copy of it.

After lunch, I asked if I could see where he did his composing, and, rather surprised by this question, Brian toddled off along the corridor, with me in tow, to a small room which contained a small desk, the top of which was inclined at an angle on which was manuscript paper containing detailed music sketches in pencil. I asked what this music was, but Brian did not reply clearly. Instead, he showed me the score of his Fourteenth Symphony, and I was surprised at how few pages it seemed to occupy. Brian also asked me why I wanted to see where he wrote music, and I replied that I had always been interested to see the places where great music had been written. Brian, I remember, looked at me for a moment over the top of his spectacles, and half smiled. "I like coming here," he said, "because it gives me a chance to get away from Mrs Brian." "Oh," I replied, not knowing quite what to say, but I do not think his remark was meant maliciously. After all, from my point of view, my presence there was due entirely to Mrs Brian's initiative.

We went back to the living-room, and I mentioned the tape-recorder I had brought with me. I had hoped that we might be able to get something down, but Brian demurred; I think the idea was not entirely unappealing to him, but he did not feel like answering questions about his earlier life. At that time, I knew nothing of his private circumstances – and, frankly, could not have cared less about them – but it was only later that I got to know him much better and how he felt that on this first visit, not knowing me, he was not prepared to answer questions. He saw my disappointment, but said, "Perhaps next time, when you come."

I was much encouraged by this remark for, from the awkward-ness that both of us felt in the early stages of this visit, we had – despite our sixty-odd years difference in ages – struck up some kind of accord. Brian, on learning that I had no intention of pressing him to answer questions on tape, was soon in a much more open frame of mind; we spoke on a wide variety of subjects including my joining the Army, which – unusually, I thought – seemed to interest him, and at about 2.30 the postman called with a delivery. Brian went to the door; "Hello, postie," he cried, in that soft, faintly Midlands, voice of his, and handed the mail to Mrs Brian. At around three o'clock he asked the time of my train. I told him, and he telephoned for a cab for me. When it came, we bade goodbye, his face now smiling in friendship, his grip firm and strong.

I returned home in a mood of some elation: my disappoint-ment at not being able to interview him was far outweighed by having met the great man at last, and having been invited to visit him again. I wrote a letter to the Brians, thanking them for their kindness during my visit and over the next month or six weeks we exchanged several letters on a variety of subjects, including the Army. I had written to Robert Simpson, some days after my visiting Brian, telling him of how I had got on and of some of the things about which Brian and I had talked. Amongst these was the fact that there was another Brian Symphony about which, it seemed, no-body knew. Brian's First Symphony, the 'Fantastic', had been written in 1907, but was effectively no more; the 'Gothic' was Brian's Second Symphony: it says so on the published score. When I told Brian how surprised I was at learning of him now having composed his Symphony No 14, he replied that there was a

First Meetings

Fifteenth, the 'Sinfonia Tragica', which was not numbered. Simpson's response a week or ten days later was full of excitement: he did not know of the 'Tragica' but there was a real No 15, which Brian had composed in the few weeks since my visit! This must have been the very work, the sketches of which I had seen on Brian's composing-desk. Simpson said he was sure that the interest now being shown in Brian's music by various people was acting as a spur to the old man – though I am sure the phrase 'old man' was not used, because I do not think either Simpson or I – or anyone else, for that matter – ever thought of Brian as being old in the generally accepted sense.

Amongst the various people who were determined to do something about Brian's music was the Australian conductor, Bryan Fairfax. This gifted musician had formed the Wind Music Society and put on some enterprising concerts including the premieres of several fine works: Alun Hoddinott's First Piano Concerto for Piano and Wind Orchestra, one of this underrated composer's masterpieces, David Dorward's Concerto for Wind and Percussion and Duane Davidson's 'Jazz Implications' – I remember these works especially. In addition, Bryan Fairfax had formed from the Wind Music Society the Polyphonia Symphony Orchestra, principally to give a hearing to major works which had been ignored. Amongst these was Mahler's Third Symphony, of which Fairfax conducted the first British performance at this time. His was a magnificent reading, although aspects of the orchestral playing – not the wind – left something to be desired. Nor is this being wise after the event. In 1954 Bruno Walter was to have come to London to give Mahler's Third Symphony at the Festival Hall, and I was to have taken part in this, in the boys' chorus. We choirboys rehearsed for many weeks, finding it difficult to pitch the opening Fs from the previous low chord. No recording of the work existed, not even at the BBC, and I remember that finding this F was a problem for us boys at first. However, I became fascinated by Mahler at this time; I had just heard the – what turned out to be rather poor – first LP recording of Mahler's First Symphony, by the Minneapolis Orchestra conducted by Dmitri Mitropoulos, and on my Saturday forays into town, I bought second-hand scores eventually of the first five Mahler symphonies, having saved up a lot of pocket-money. I thought that by knowing rather more about Mahler's Third Symphony than my fellow-choristers, it would help me in the proposed performance. But after quite a few weeks, we learned that Bruno Walter would be unable to come to London, and the performance never took place.

I knew Mahler's Symphony No 3 well enough by the end of the decade to judge the Polyphonia performance better than many people there. Whilst I was thrilled to hear it live, it was not until I obtained Charles Adler's Vienna recording that the work made its full and proper impact on me. I do not wish to denigrate the achievements of Bryan Fairfax; I remember a revelatory Bruckner Festival he directed, including the most penetrating account of Bruckner's Second Symphony I have ever heard, and a deeply impressive slow movement in a fine reading of Bruckner's Symphony No 8, with the works illuminatingly introduced by Robert Simpson. When it became clear in the early months of 1960 that Fairfax intended to put on the 'Gothic', I thought it time I saw the score for myself.

By this time I was in the Army; at first, I played an administrative role in the Royal Tournament in June, and, stationed for a while in and near London, I was keen to assist in the 'Gothic' perform-

First Meetings

ance. In my Army uniform, I went with Geoffrey Lee Cooper to meet with Fairfax and some other people and undertook to do what I could. But within the next month, two things occurred to cause me to withdraw from giving help to this project. The first was my visiting the British Museum and studying the two-volume score of the 'Gothic', which the Museum had had since January, 1934. It became clear to me that a largely amateur performance of this staggeringly demanding composition was not one which the work required – I felt that a largely amateur performance would very likely militate against the symphony, not so much the orchestral movements as the choral ones. My opinion came from my own singing experience.

The second was that, as a result of my Army training, I found myself adept at several things of great use in certain circumstances – I was able to shin up and down a rope at speed, I was good at night camouflage and I was also quite good at close-quarter combat with a knife. I had also qualified as a marksman on the sub-machine gun. It so happened that within a few weeks in the summer of 1960, I was chosen for a strategic operation which required some secrecy.

I had therefore to withdraw from giving any help, which, because of my Army commitments, would have been less than I would have hoped, to Bryan Fairfax and his people in respect of their 'Gothic' performance; what made it particularly galling was that the confidential nature of the operation for which I had been selected meant I could not explain my decision. I was unwilling to say then that the extraordinarily heroic efforts which Fairfax was prepared to make in the cause of this great work would, in my opinion, probably not serve the 'Gothic' in the long run. This symphony, it still seems to me, cries out for committed perform-

HAVERGAL BRIAN

ances by nothing less than world-class professional orchestras.

I visited Brian again in the summer of 1960; this second visit was much more relaxed and friendly than the first; I was delighted that Brian met me at the door and was genuinely pleased to see me. I remember his smile to this day. This visit was notable for Brian doing something that he had not done before: he was keen to show me his latest work, the Symphony No 16, which he had just completed. I spent some time looking through it with him, and noticed a calligraphic point that I adopted for my own music: whilst the notes and indications were in black ink, the bar-lines were in a lighter blue ball-point. This made the score much easier to read and I commented on this to Brian. I think he was quite pleased, for there is no doubt that he took some little trouble with the appearance of his scores – as, indeed, every composer should.

But the Sixteenth Symphony was the main subject of our discussions; Brian pointed to a passage, heavily but not overpoweringly scored, in medium-slow tempo, of which he was clearly proud. I remember his words vividly: "I think that's one of the best things I've done," showing me two pages especially, moving towards a section in 7/4 tempo. Malcolm MacDonald, on Page 57 of Volume II of his study of the Brian symphonies, quotes the remark where I am referred to as 'Robert Walker', the name, of course, by which I was then known. I adopted 'Robert Matthew-Walker' later to avoid confusion with another 'Robert Walker' a talented younger composer born in 1946 who had joined PRS before me: confusingly, our compositions were handled by the same publisher, Basil Ramsey, and, more confusingly still, after I had joined RCA Records in London, the 'other Robert Walker' later joined the small record company Prelude and produced a number of albums includ-

First Meetings

ing several of British music, as I did!

There is a further point concerning Malcolm MacDonald's analytical comments on Brian's Sixteenth Symphony; he mentions the 'warlike' nature of much of the composition and sought clues as to its provenance: Brian often asked about Army life from me as the work was apparently gestating in his mind; so it seems 'warlike' elements had been in his thoughts. I asked Brian about the processes in his music: how he actually composed. He replied that an idea would come into his head, without bidding and as voices, always voices. It would be a fragment, and would often be the beginning of a work, which he would set down and think over, and work at. I remember him saying, "It is like a headache and you have to get rid of it. In my case, I have to write it down, and it goes on from there, you see." I remember Brian saying something to me during this visit, which I think he also said to Robert Simpson on another occasion. I forget the precise nature of the conversation at that point, but what he said hit me like a thunderbolt. It was a paradox: "Nothing matters. Nothing matters," he said. "But always remember that even the least, insignificant thing is important."

It was either during this visit or the next one, which occurred a few weeks later, that we talked on Shostakovich's Eighth Symphony, which had been broadcast a week or so before. At that time, the work was hardly known in England: this may have been the symphony's first airing in the United Kingdom for quite a few years. Luckily, I had heard it, and we both shared some enthusiasm for it; I remember Brian saying he thought it a better symphony than Shostakovich's Tenth, and that he regarded the Eighth as the best work by Shostakovich he had heard. I asked him how he felt his music differed from Shostakovich's: "With me", he replied, "it is

HAVERGAL BRIAN

a combination of moods; that is the way it seems to work."

On my next visit a week or so later we discussed opera. Brian was full of the live television broadcast a few days before, direct from Rome, of Verdi's 'Otello' which was, I believe, the first such telecast. "Did you see it?" he asked, but I told him I was able only to snatch most of Act I before my fellow-soldiers came in to force me to switch over to 'Take Your Pick' or some other programme. We agreed that Act I was Verdi at his greatest (a view shared by another British composer, George Lloyd, who told me that Verdi's use of the orchestra in this act should be studied by everyone who wanted to become an operatic composer) but Brian much amused me when he reported what Mrs Brian had said.

Excited by the announcement in *Radio Times* of this telecast, Brian had settled down in readiness, but as the opera was about to start, Mrs Brian got up and said she was going out. "Why don't you watch this?" Brian asked her. "I don't want to," she said. "But it's a very great masterpiece, and you may not get another chance like this." "I don't care," she replied, "and in any case I don't like opera." With that, she left to go and visit a neighbour, and Brian watched the opera alone. "I daren't tell her that I've got five operas of my own in the cupboard – if she knew that, she'd probably throw them all out to the dustman!"

I asked him about his operas, and he went through them with me, pointing out that his one-act 'Agamemnon' was a setting in English intended as a curtain-raiser for Richard Strauss's 'Elektra', "To explain what had happened before Elektra begins, you see." His "you see" was very typical of him when he spoke of his own music. As a result of the 'Otello' broadcast I asked him if he watched much television; his answer was unforgettable: "No; television

First Meetings

glorifies nobodies."

I think on this visit Brian asked me if I knew of Douglas Glass, the photographer – I was reminded of my father's north country origins when Brian, using the short vowel, asked "Is this Glass fellow any good?" I said that I knew of his work, had seen many photographic portraits by him of musicians and in my opinion he was one of the best photographers working in that field. It transpired that Glass had arranged to come to Shoreham to take photographs of Brian, who had not heard of him.

I regret I did not discuss Brian's own operas much with him; I was more interested in his symphonies and his other current work. I was also concerned that it seemed as though no established British publishing company wanted much to do with him. It was true that Schotts handled the scores of some of his symphonies on a hire basis: I had obtained one of the Eighth in this way, but I found it extraordinary that I was handed a manuscript by the composer himself, not even a photocopy. It must be remembered that in those days photocopying was not at all what it has since become and expensive 'dyelines' took a long time to make, giving off a hideous chemical aroma during processing that was possibly also harmful. Copies of scores could not be made quickly; even so, I found being given the composer's manuscript as I came in off the street to be a chastening experience. I took it to Brian to seek clarification of one point, and, seeing his own manuscript, he told me to take care of the score and return it safely to Schotts – which, needless to say, I did.

In 1989 I became managing director of the music publishers Alfred Lengnick & Co Ltd, and acquired all of Robert Simpson's then unpublished works, together with others on which he was working, thereby 'bringing him back into the fold' so to speak, of Lengnick, his first publisher. I was anxious to find out about the fate of Brian's music, so far as publishing it was concerned. I telephoned Malcolm MacDonald who told me that United Music Publishers had taken over Brian's works. I was on the one hand disappointed not to be able to obtain any of Brian's scores for Lengnick, but pleased that his works had found an established publisher. I could only feel sad that, were it not for the courage of Graham Hatton, who founded Musica Viva and was able to issue study facsimile scores of several of Brian's late symphonies, a great British composer should have been taken up by Cranz and Schott – both major German publishing houses – and therefore initially had been utterly ignored by important British publishers. Today, all Brian's works are handled by United Music Publishers, who took over Cranz and Musica Viva; at last, the music of a great British composer is handled by a great British publishing company.

Chapter III
The 'Gothic' Performed

My third visit to Havergal Brian that summer was to be my last for some time, for my Army career perforce had to take precedence. But I found myself still able to compose in my few quiet moments and I began a Cello Concerto which quoted directly from Brian's Eleventh Symphony (the opening unison horn theme of the second movement); when I showed this to Robert Simpson he was very much taken aback at the quotation, which was a kind of musical 'objet trouvé' rather than an organic section. I destroyed the score.

A year later the strategic operation in which I had been involved had come to an end, and I was stationed in Aldershot prior to moving to the Joint Air Reconnaissance Intelligence Centre in Huntingdon before my final posting to the War Office in Whitehall. On June 21st, 1961 I read in *The Times* an article on the 'Gothic' Symphony ("from a correspondent" as the then genteel newspaper had it – I was certain I recognised Robert Simpson's distinctive prose-style in the piece); three days later, I was at the Westminster Methodist Central Hall to hear the first performance of the 'Gothic' with an Army colleague.

Although some of my misgivings proved correct as to the standard of the choral performance, and some of the choral singing was unfortunate, there was no doubt in my mind that Bryan Fairfax had excelled himself and had brought off an extraordinary triumph. My fears were not all realised, I am glad to say, although I recall that there seemed to be a problem with the harps: I believe there was none at all. Fairfax had managed to raise the funds to mount the performance, the programme of which was adorned with what I consider to be the best Brian photograph by Douglas Glass, taken in August, 1960. The programme also contained a list of the Subscribers to the Havergal Brian Fund, which included, amongst many others, W.W. Johnson, founder of the National Federation of Gramophone Societies and the gentle Don Mather on behalf of the Music Club, several of whose members – including the remarkable couple, Ken and Madeline Golder – were also present. Amongst other subscribers was the British National Party.

I spoke briefly with Brian and Robert Simpson and their wives prior to the performance, wishing Brian luck, but I think he was on another planet: not that he should have paid much attention to me but, although he was pleased to see me, he had a kind of what can only be described as an 'other-worldly' air about him. I had never seen it before, nor did I see it again. You can imagine the feelings of those present as Brian himself, rather gingerly, made his way down some steps to take his bow at the end of the performance. Fairfax, as the applause began, turned directly to his right, arm raised, and summoned the composer. I freely confess I had tears in my eyes, and I suspect I was not the only one.

That evening, I saw composers as diverse as Malcolm Arnold and Sir Eugène Goossens, amongst others, and I understand that David Dorward was there and was introduced to Brian by Robert Simpson. Goossens had sent Brian a telegram wishing luck for the performance, which Brian did not receive until a week or so later. He wrote to Goossens on July 3rd:

"My dear Sir Eugène,

Better late than never! Many sincere thanks for your greetings telegram which I have now received. It was an honour to have you at the 'Gothic' after all our hopes and wishes and memories of those who had hoped to hear it. Yours affectionately, Havergal"

Goossens replied on August 12th:

"My dear old friend,

I feel very guilty at not having answered your note. I cannot tell you how thrilled I was to be at the performance of your great work. Naturally I had a tremendous 'family' interest in it, for you probably guess how much the saying that 'hope deferred maketh the heart sick' applied to my feelings of frustration at never being able to give the Symphony in America.

Its splendid performance under Fairfax, whom you were lucky to have in command, convinced me more than ever how great a conception 'The Gothic' is. It has stood the test of time wonderfully, for nothing in it sounded dated and indeed many of the orchestral ideas were tremendously contemporary in feeling, especially in the scherzo.

It must not be allowed to suffer the fate of most New English works of big scale and languish many more years for a second performance. I shall continue to urge, as I have done all along, that it be quickly performed again with, if possible, the same resources and a more suitable hall so that the public may realise the importance of the work you conceived. I know something of the difficulties of getting further performances of major sized works. My own two Operatoria [*sic*] 'Apocalypse' and both my Symphonies are well on the way to being forgotten for lack of further performance.

Anyway, you must have felt the other evening the reward for your devoted labours and how it spontaneously sprang from an enthralled audience. Keep the good work going and I hope to see you one day either in London or in your own home territory. Your affectionate, Eugène".

Six days later, Brian replied:

"My dear Old Friend,
Your letter was a joy and unexpected and more so for only a few days ago – having felt suspended since the Gothic, I came to earth in your recent broadcast Prom Concert, and greatly enjoyed your Ravel and the Roussel Symphony [No 3] – I went to bed quite happy.

As you say it was (Gothic) a family affair and in looking back to the years of my boyhood when I heard operas under your grandfather with the Carl Rosa and your father with the Moody Manners and the B.N.O.C. [British National Opera Company] – it stretches over a very long period. As regards the Gothic the performance owed much to your championship of it years ago and we were lucky to hear it under the fearless Fairfax.

Affectionately yours, Havergal."

A day or so after receiving this reply, on August 26th, 1961, Goossens called unannounced at Brian's home. The next day, Brian wrote to Goossens:

The 'Gothic' Performed

"My dear old friend,

What a pleasant surprise yesterday – how I wish I had known beforehand for in this world of Shoreham Beach shingle one dresses anyhow. It is a primitive place thrown up by the sea for ages, and now being turned into habitation. I prefer the green fields and woods of my early life and birth – but the Rent Act altered things for us. We ought to have had a quiet sit down and talk – for after you had left I realised my "slipping on the stepping stones" for I meant I hated the journey from here to London, or talked of your famous Poems as 'Pieces' – well, well – things happen in old age – the suppressed excitement of finding you at the door – when I was alone. Someday we will meet again. As ever, affectionately, Havergal"

This letter was answered by Goossens on September 2nd:

"My dear Havergal,

It was grand to see you in Shoreham and I hope you have forgiven my intrusion. I was pleasantly surprised to even find you at home, and certainly did not expect to find you dressed in formal attire! Gerald Cockshott who is Treasurer of the Composers' Guild and your near neighbour in Mill Hill Drive, Shoreham, was proud and pleased to have the unexpected pleasure of meeting you. Sometime later on we must get together and I will write ahead to warn you. Affectionately as ever, Eugène Goossens"

Brian replied on October 6th, a long time to answer a letter for him:

"My dear Eugène,

It will be a fine occasion when we meet sometime in the future here. At present my wife and I are rather disturbed for we are expecting my youngest daughter and her family from Africa before [the] end of this month and – we are going to be crowded. When we were bedevilled at Harrow by the rent act – our younger [sic] daughter and her husband bought this place to relieve us of troubles and uncertainties.

I suppose you have read Cardus on your old friend Tommy [Beecham, who had died on March 8th 1961. Neville Cardus had published 'Sir Thomas Beecham: A memoir' by the time Brian wrote this letter]. I could have supplemented it for I had much to do in helping him between 1908 and 1911. He was a phenomenon. Affectionately as ever, Havergal."

Brian and Goossens did not meet again; Sir Eugène Goossens, already a sick man when he last saw Brian, died eight months later.

The critical response to the 'Gothic' was not really up to the work itself. Today, when symphonies by Mahler and Bruckner are considered good box-office, and are in the repertoires of all major orchestras and conductors, one must remember that in 1961 the idea of listening to a vast symphony of the duration of the 'Gothic' was so wholly unusual that the general concert-going public, including critics, was simply not used to hearing works of such length. But it was, of course, the first time that anyone had heard this music: the impossibility of forming a considered opinion upon a single hearing, of this of all works, was shown by many of the press notices.

As I have said, by the end of 1961 I had transferred to the War Office in Whitehall where I met a retired Colonel who had served in World War I, F. Felgate Stone. He was employed in the same Directorate as I, and Colonel Stone was quite interested in music.

The 'Gothic' Performed

One day, I mentioned my friendship with Brian to him; I shall never forget Colonel Stone's reaction. He had clearly heard the unusual surname before and the next day he told me that for some months during World War I, whilst waiting to be drafted to France, he had encountered a "Bill Brian", a private in the camp where he was based, who sometimes played the piano in the mess – a selection of music-hall songs – for other soldiers and who was soon discharged from the Army for a medical condition. Colonel Stone said he recalled that this "Private Bill Brian" had a shock of red hair and was a bit of an "awkward cuss". Havergal Brian's first name was William; Brian had been invalided out of the Army after a few months.

In February, 1962 Bryan Fairfax conducted the premiere of Brian's Eighteenth Symphony at St Pancras Town Hall, which had been written for him and the Polyphonia Symphony Orchestra. The score of the Eighteenth had been displayed at the Central Hall on the night of the 'Gothic' premiere, and the work was played as part of the opening concert of that year's St Pancras Arts Festival by what was described as "polyphonia workshop" – perhaps indicating that a less than fully-professional performance could be expected. The programme included Busoni's Piano Concerto with Philip Levi as the soloist. Fairfax himself wrote the programme note, which struck me as being just right for the newcomer; he spoke of the work possessing "something of the essential spirit of the march...direct, concise, purposeful".

I was there and heard the first of the late symphonies Brian had written since I had met him. With the best will in the world, I became more convinced than ever that these intellectually and technically demanding, concentrated and utterly unique scores

51

Opening of Havergal Brian's Tenth Symphony (1954),
from the composer's manuscript.

The 'Gothic' Performed

could not properly be realised by an orchestra merely assembled for one concert or another, no matter if professionals took part. Brian had, it seemed, made little or no compromises; the performance was simply not good enough. I spoke with Brian and his wife afterwards, but what could I say?

The following month I left the War Office and returned to civilian life. I was dissatisfied with much of the music I had written up to then, with the exception of my first three symphonies and one or two other shorter works, and wanted to put everything I had into two biggish compositions. In the Army, I planned a full-scale setting of the Mass for large double chorus and orchestra, and a Fourth Symphony, a lighter work, both of which I intended to write on my release. I completed the Kyrie of the Mass in 1962, the day before I learned of the existence of Britten's 'War Requiem'. Whilst my work was not a 'Requiem' I waited until I had heard Britten's score before settling down to the 'Gloria', for which I had what I thought were several good ideas. I was as moved by the Britten work as I had been by the 'Gothic' the year before, but amazed by Brian's anticipation in the 'Gothic' of aspects of the 'War Requiem', particularly in the relative treatment in both works of the soprano soloist against a large choir, and between Figures 124 and 131 of the 'Gothic's' Te Deum and Britten's setting of the Hosanna. What were hailed by Britten devotees to be examples of Britten's originality had actually been presaged by Brian more than 30 years earlier, and although the 'War Requiem' was completed after the 'Gothic' premiere, there is no way that Britten would have been aware of Brian's music. I was even more struck in 1963 by Brian's anticipation, in his setting of 'Aeterna fac cum sanctis' (Figures 265/7) and the sound and texture of Britten's 'Cantata Misericordium'.

I had decided to postpone the rest of my Mass for the time being. What I needed was a fresh perspective on my own music, and I put most of my thoughts into a longish letter to Brian. I did not mince my words on the shortcomings of the 'Gothic' performance, nor on the orchestral standard of performance his Eighteenth Symphony had received.

He replied on June 17th, 1962:

"Dear Robert Walker,

So you are out of the Army. I suppose things seem different to you now that you are out of the distinguishing clothes of a Soldier. You will be glad to return to your music – though from what you told me you were not too restricted when in the Army. I am sure that I do not in any way correspond in looks, hair colour or what not with your friend's Brian of the Army. [In all of these things, Brian did correspond!]

I was not so careless when in the Army as to disclose my identity as a musician for I found the Army very different from what I had imagined – and the one thing which impressed me more than any other was that we were at War. As to what you disliked about the Gothic performance – it would have been more electric with professionals – but on the other hand the performance aroused a great interest from many unexpected quarters and must have prepared a ready response for another performance – though often memories are short-lived. Considering that all the printed parts of the Gothic (orchestral) were lost and that it had to start from scratch in mss parts, I think that all honour is due to Bryan Fairfax and Dr Robert Simpson – who was undoubtedly at the back of it. Very largely a professional performance depends on Dr Simpson for only the BBC can afford the financial outlay – they contributed generously to the original performance at Westminster last June.

Again the 18th Symphony would have sounded very different with an established professional orchestra. Enthusiasm can go a long way but it cannot displace or equal the security and excellence of a professional body. Half a loaf is better than no bread – if it does not create misunderstandings. Again that performance at St Pancras (by the way, who was St Pancras? – the nearest I can get to it is the Latin noun Cras – tomorrow) was due entirely to Bryan Fairfax who is tireless and one can only hope he will get the professional orchestra which he deserves. Yours sincerely, Havergal Brian."

I replied, telling him about St Pancras, and of my other works, and on June 25th Brian wrote back:

"Dear Robert Walker,
Thank you for your letter. I am always pleased to hear from you when you tell me of your musical activities, so I can really wish your continuance of your Mass and other projects and hope that one day you will succeed in a public performance. You have a good friend in Dr Simpson to whom you should request his criticism and help of your Mass when complete. My friendship with Dr Simpson began in a curious way. I had been to the BBC to leave my 9th Symphony with Mr Eric Warr and just as I was leaving Dr Simpson entered the building. Mr Warr said, "This is Havergal Brian; he has just left me his 9th Symphony". That is how the interest in my Symphonies began & performances followed. The BBC have other Symphonies of mine 13,14,15,16,17,19 and the 18th has been sent them by Bryan Fairfax. When Mr Fairfax was working on the 18th

HAVERGAL BRIAN

– I was working on my 20th. Longer than the previous, it plays for 36 minutes. So far I have not finished a copy of the score. Also last April-May I wrote a short Comedy Overture. I have made copies of my recent Symphonies – I should advise you to do the same. All good luck, Havergal Brian."

Having decided to abandon my Mass, I was now determined to proceed with the Symphony No 4 which I completed before the end of the Summer of 1962 and which I had mentioned to Brian in my letter of circa June 20th – which makes sense of his comment "I have made copies of my recent Symphonies – I should advise you to do the same." Not for the first time in a letter, Brian overstated the duration of an unperformed work: his Twentieth Symphony plays not for thirty-six minutes, but for twenty-five.

Brian's letter of June 25th clears up, to some degree, the date of composition of his Twentieth Symphony – "When Mr Fairfax was working on the 18th – I was working on my 20th." The preparations and rehearsals for the premiere of the Eighteenth Symphony took place mostly in the first six weeks of 1962, when Bryan Fairfax would have been "working" on it. It has generally been thought that Brian did not begin the Twentieth Symphony until March 1962, but his letter clearly proves otherwise.

56

Chapter IV
Further Contact

After the premiere of Havergal Brian's Symphony No 18 there followed a period of four-and-a-half years during which none of his works was publicly performed or broadcast: why? I felt strongly that the largely amateur performances of the 'Gothic' and the Eighteenth Symphony had indeed tended to "create misunderstandings", as Brian had put in one of his letters. In several quarters, it seemed as though having finally heard the legendary 'Gothic', alongside half-a-dozen earlier broadcasts – the break in BBC broadcasts of Brian's music at this time was almost seven years – his music either did not capture public imagination, or was critically perceived not to come up to the levels claimed for it.

So far as the BBC was concerned, Robert Simpson was still there, but the important and all-influential post of the organisation's Controller, Music had, at the end of 1959, passed to William (later, Sir William) Glock, who was new to the BBC and brought with him a host of ideas for programming, of which among the more important to him was the opening up to British ears of the work of the Second Viennese School, which had indeed been much neglected by the BBC. He also cut down the length of programmes at the Promenade Concerts, a move brought in to raise orchestral standards by devoting more rehearsal time to each work – which,

HAVERGAL BRIAN

in the short and medium terms, may have been beneficial in that regard. But it seemed to many people, myself included, that a number of exceptionally gifted composers, whose music was of great significance and which had been broadcast quite regularly and performed by the BBC's orchestras in the recent past, were now virtually ignored. Amongst the many composers who suffered in this way were: Carlo Martelli – one of the most gifted British composers of his generation (he was born in 1935 – a story of neglect almost as strange as that of Havergal Brian); Richard Arnell (like Brian, another Beecham protégé); Stanley Bate – a tragic figure, whose Third Symphony is a masterpiece; and York Bowen – his Third Symphony, Horn Concerto and Sinfonietta Concertante for Brass and Orchestra are thrilling works. These are just a few examples from a reasonably lengthy list of British composers, which included – in the early years of Glock's regime – Havergal Brian.

For myself, I had decided to pursue a commercial career and although I wrote to Brian occasionally I did not visit him for some time. But whatever internal battles at the BBC were being fought on Brian's behalf (and I have no inside knowledge of these, or indeed if they "were being fought" – but, knowing Robert Simpson's character, I should imagine they were), 1966 proved to be a very important year for Brian and the BBC. I twice saw him at the Albert Hall in 1966 – for the Prom performance of the Twelfth Symphony on August 4th, and in October for Boult's 'Gothic'.

Brian's Twelfth Symphony began the programme; the second item was the world premiere of Gordon Crosse's 'Ceremony' for cello and orchestra – particularly bad programme planning. The Symphony – a very fine account under Norman Del Mar – was the

58

Further Contact

first work of his own Brian had heard at a Prom for 31 years, since Sir Henry Wood had given Brian's *Festal Dance* (the original finale to the Fantastic Symphony of 1907) at Queen's Hall on September 30th, 1935. Wood's performance of the *Festal Dance* was with the BBC Symphony Orchestra, not the Queen's Hall Orchestra as has been sometimes erroneously stated, and came at the end of a programme – the tenth item, in fact, after an all-Wagner first half – the length of which concert certainly would seem to justify Glock's later reforms in that regard. Brian's work was the only piece in the concert that did not have a programme note – Rosa Newmarch had written on all the other items. The *Festal Dance* was noted in the programme with merely the title and no indication as to whether Brian was alive or not.

The Boult performance of the 'Gothic' on October 30th was easily the finest this work has had. The BBC had at last done the composer proud; the BBC2 classical television programme 'Music International' showed a lengthy film on Brian, 'The Unknown Warrior of Music' on October 27th introduced by Bernard Keeffe, and by way of previewing the performance, Simpson wrote enthusiastically about the work in the *Radio Times*:

"Come to the Royal Albert Hall if you can! This is the gigantic and legendary score that Beecham, Wood, Harty and Goossens all wanted to conduct, but for which they could never get the resources; that Tovey declared a great work; that Strauss called 'magnificent'. It is a chance in a lifetime to hear this largest symphony ever written – it is so immense that Havergal Brian, when he wrote it after the first world war, never expected to hear it. Now when he is a vigorous ninety, and just finishing his Twenty-seventh Symphony, he will be with us at the Albert Hall. And I hope a large audience will hail this formidable and heroic figure in English music.

He has spent his long life in retiring dedication to his art, placing each completed work on one side, to go on with the next, without much thought of performance or accolades. He is a very original composer, yet profoundly human, and if we value music that can move us, we cannot afford to neglect his like.

You will not find the Gothic Symphony drily cerebral or abstruse; you will find it full of grandeur, beauty, depth, and striking individuality. It is direct music of great architectural stature and compelling force; its vastness is not mere megalomania – it is matched by inner strength and an imaginative scope that dictates the scale. In the mighty Te Deum that forms its extended climax there are colossal sounds, but the greatest stroke is the wonderful mysterious end, abjuring all uproar. Restraint, variety of sound, fantastic power – the work has them all. It is tremendous music and the sound of 700 performers and the brass orchestras will make its immediate impact."

Who would not wish to be present at such a work after reading this? Pierre Boulez was conducting Beethoven's 'Choral' at the Festival Hall on the same night yet a large audience came to the Albert Hall and listened to the 'Gothic' – with rapt attention, as the recording shows. I had the most profound admiration for Boult's command of this fearsome score, and the reception accorded to Brian himself was deeply moving. Deryck Cooke contributed a fine programme note for the Boult performance – Simpson had written that for the Fairfax premiere – and it seemed to me that if musicians

Further Contact

of the calibre of Richard Strauss, Donald Francis Tovey, Henry Wood, Eugène Goossens, Hamilton Harty, Adrian Boult, Robert Simpson, Deryck Cooke and Harold Truscott – amongst others – had been excited by the power of the music purely from the score alone, then, quite apart from what my own ears told me, I would rather follow their judgement than that of commentators such as Colin Mason, whose "notice" in *The Daily Telegraph* of this Boult performance was one of the worst pieces of journalistic ignorance it has ever been my misfortune to read. Robert Simpson told me of an encounter he had had after the last Boult rehearsal with a critic for a major newspaper: this so depressed me, and left me convinced that the work would never get a fair hearing in some quarters. *The Times* critic said he was bewildered; so was I, having read his review, as he referred to things in the score which do not exist! I wondered if he was at the performance. Luckily, the press was not all bad: Edward Greenfield in *The Guardian* reacted much more positively now to the work than he had at the time of the Fairfax performance.

Brian had now seen it all: decades of neglect followed by purblind misunderstanding in some quarters. I rather naively thought that, no matter what, he would always be around; when I saw him on that October evening, I could not believe he was 90 years old. He seemed immortal to me, as he did the last time I saw him, which was in July, 1967.

A friend of mine, 'Jim' Fuller, whom I met when he joined the Music Club in the early 1960s, learned of the Club's connexion with Brian and later floored me by saying that he was sure he had seen Brian conduct. Jim was a most remarkable man: profession-ally, he was a quantity surveyor who had – exceptionally – played competitive baseball in England in the 1930s and was also a qualified hockey referee. He died in 1993 at the age of 94 having been a keen opera and concert-goer since World War I. He kept many programmes and was certain that he had seen Brian conduct a work of his own in the early 1920s. I wrote to Brian, mentioning Jim Fuller, and Brian invited us down for July 12th.

Brian gave me a great welcome, and was most kind to Jim: he called Mrs Brian to "bring cider for the lads" which she did. He looked rosy-cheeked and extremely well, wearing an open-neck cricket shirt with cravat (the first time I had seen him without his customary bow-tie), and some natty fawn trousers. He complained about "a touch of deafness on bad days, but luckily they were not often" – and this day was a good one.

He was most interested to hear of Jim Fuller's daughter Yvonne, who had been a pupil of Oda Slobodskaya and Lotte Lehmann and had appeared at the Proms in Parsifal under Boulez, amongst many other engagements. Brian bade Jim to enquire at Chesters and Augeners for the early songs of his that they had published and said he hoped Yvonne would find some and "sing them with my blessing." This was the first time I heard Brian talk of his pre-Gothic music. He spoke of the recent broadcast of his Fifth Symphony – the old numbering of *Das Siegeslied* now known as No 4 – which I had also heard and which had much impressed me: the concentrated power especially, although it seemed there might have been shortcomings in the performance.

Jim Fuller had attended the Boult performance of the 'Gothic' the previous year and asked Brian about the use of the birdscare in that score. Brian said the birdscare was introduced as a memory of his younger years in Sussex, of early morning walks over the Downs. I found this a remarkable reply. Jim was a great Sussex man,

Further Contact

and in his early days had met and befriended Sir Adrian Boult and his wife on their honeymoon. It so transpired that Jim's memory was indeed accurate after 46 years: he held Brian, Mrs Brian and me enthralled at his description of seeing Brian conduct the *Fantastic Variations on an Old Rhyme* in Brighton with strong, demonstrative gestures in 1921, describing the clothes Brian wore on the rostrum: a dark brown, three-piece tweed suit with cream breast pocket handkerchief and matching tie. Brian appeared well pleased as he told us of having recently been awarded an honorary D.Mus. from Manchester University, although he did not go to receive it in person: "It was awarded in absentia," he said with satisfaction, and in answer to Jim's question as to whom he considered the best of the younger British composers he cited Simpson, Tippett and John Gardner, and of the younger conductors he mentioned Norman Del Mar, Stanley Pope and Leonard Bernstein, whose televised performance of Mahler's Eighth Symphony from the Royal Albert Hall in April 1966 had impressed him. At that time, of course, I had no idea of any part I might play in trying to persuade Bernstein to consider performing the 'Gothic'.

Brian had recently drafted his Twenty-ninth Symphony which he said he was "just going to finish off". I assumed he meant the full score, as he showed us what he had completed of it. On reading Malcolm MacDonald's analysis of the Twenty-ninth in his book, there is no doubt that its mood was that of the man we saw that day.

His mood was calm, happy and seemingly content. I had never quite seen him like this before, at peace with the world, and certainly felt that there was more music in him. I was astounded when he told Jim he had had ideas for a new Cello Concerto and two string quartets – which never materialised – and on this ebullient upbeat note we took our leave of him, giving Mrs Brian a lift to the shops en route, with Brian waving us goodbye at the door.

Towards the end of 1969 I got married, and wrote to Brian telling him of this; his reply was rather odd, hoping that my "excursion into marriage would be more successful than that of others" – I was puzzled until after his death I was told something of the nature of his marital affairs.

Chapter V
A Passing Tribute

In 1970 I joined the British record business, following a career in the City for most of the previous decade after studies in Paris with Darius Milhaud. My first company was CBS, and within three months of joining them I was appointed head of the Classical Department in London, my predecessor being Bill Newman. To succeed me in my first job there I managed to persuade Ray Burford, my old Music Club colleague, to join CBS as Classical Sales Manager, where I knew his outstanding ability as a salesman and his considerable knowledge of music and records would be a dynamic combination.

One of my aims was to try to bring Brian's music to the attention of major artists, and I thought that Leonard Bernstein would be the man to do the 'Gothic'. In 1972, Bernstein came to Britain, when I met him for the first time. He was here for performances of Mahler's Second Symphony, which he recorded for CBS (for the second time) and performed the work at the Edinburgh Festival and in Ely Cathedral for television. I had written a long internal memorandum to CBS's UK managing director, M. Richard ('Dick') Asher, and his co-director Maurice Oberstein ('Obie') – the latter being one of the greatest men ever to have worked in the record business – concerning recording Brian's music, and they were both positive in their response, as was CBS's Director of Masterworks Europe, Paul Myers, with whom I had discussed the memo's contents. Paul advised that the best way forward would be to try to interest Leonard Bernstein and to await developments.

My work at CBS brought me into contact with many music journalists and I got to know another enthusiast for Brian's music, Mike Thorne, who then worked on *Hi-Fi News and Record Review*, for which the blind audio engineer Angus McKenzie also wrote. Later, Mike went to live in New York to run a successful rock music recording studio in Greenwich Village. I was pleased to see Sir Michael Tippett praise Mike's Manhattan studio work in his autobiography *Those Twentieth-Century Blues*.

My wife, my mother and Mike Thorne all called me at my CBS office on the day Brian's death was announced. It was two months before what would have been his 97th birthday. Mike asked if I would contribute an essay on Brian for the journal. I decided that I should take this opportunity to produce a piece on Brian, in a publication with a monthly readership approaching a quarter of a million, which would be more in the nature of an introduction to his life and work, aimed at the inquiring newcomer, rather than a standard obituary. The essay, sub-headed "a plea for recognition of a prolific but unheard genius", appeared in the February, 1973 issue; although there are several things in it that I would express slightly differently today, and some that later events have clarified, more than twenty years later a plea for Brian's recognition still has to be made and, in some respects, is even more relevant. This is what I wrote in December, 1972:

"A creative artist's death is often the occasion for an assess-

A Passing Tribute

ment of his work, but when the majority of his output is unknown and unperformed such an assessment is much more difficult to make. It might therefore seem foolhardy to attempt such a task, but I have no hesitation in saying that I regard Havergal Brian as possibly the greatest composer this country has produced, certainly one of the greatest symphonists of this century, and a major figure who will in time be given his due.

As Brian is probably little more than a name to the vast majority of readers, I should like to give some background to the man and his music, and try to explain why I hold these views.

Havergal Brian was born on January 29th, 1876 near Dresden in Staffordshire. He left school at the age of twelve and was apprenticed for a short time in a woodyard from which he was dismissed for utilising long planks of wood he had planed as manuscript paper. Although almost entirely self-taught, he managed to pursue his studies to such an extent that he gained an appointment as a local church organist and was able to take a very active part in the musical life of his community. From an early age he wanted to be a composer, and his first works were written in the late 1890s. In the industrial Midlands and North of England at that time the choral tradition was very strong and he came into contact with many important musicians.

In the early 1900s he produced a succession of works, a concert overture *For Valour*, his first *English Suite*, a symphonic poem *Hero and Leander*, and some early choral works: *Psalm 23* for tenor, chorus and orchestra, and *Psalm 137 – By the Waters of Babylon* for baritone, chorus and orchestra, which contributed to his growing reputation as a composer. These works, together with other orchestral and choral pieces which succeeded them, led to Brian being regarded as one of the up-and-coming English composers of his generation.

At this time Brian's circumstances were such that he could not devote the whole of his working day to music. He held a position as a representative for a timber company and was able to travel about the Midlands, hearing a lot of music and also supplementing his income as a music critic. As long as he kept the orders up for his company, he was left pretty much to his own devices. In 1909 a wealthy businessman became Brian's benefactor and Brian was able to give up his job and devote all his time to composition. However, this only lasted until just before the first world war, when disagreement between the two men came to a head and his patron cut off his income.

At this time also it must be remembered that Brian was nearly 40 and had much to look forward to. However his lack of professional qualifications led him to accept a post during the war as a clerk in a munitions factory in Birmingham. It was whilst working under such circumstances that Brian produced his first opera, 'The Tigers' which, although it has never been performed (the orchestral score is lost), has been published in vocal score. Until someone does for this work what Rimsky-Korsakov did for Mussorgsky's operas (though with more fidelity to the original) it will never be performed, but a close examination reveals it to be of considerable importance, surely the first great English comic opera. [In fact, the full score of 'The Tigers' was dramatically found in the late 1970s – sixty years after it was written.]

At the end of the war Brian began work on his most notorious composition – the Gothic Symphony. This was begun in 1919 and finished, in all essentials, in 1923, but the full score was not ready

A Passing Tribute

until 1927. During the intervening period, Brian had moved to London to attempt to find work. His financial situation at this time was so desperate that this strong-willed man was reduced to contemplating suicide. He determined to buy a gun to end it all, yet on the day when he had saved enough money to buy one and went to the gunsmiths, he found it was their half-day, and the shop was closed.

The Gothic Symphony is a work of staggering dimensions. It is probably the biggest symphony in terms of numbers of performers and playing time that has ever been written, and utilises an orchestra so gigantic that each section uses every known instrument of the particular orchestral family. Part I comprises three purely instrumental movements, like Beethoven's Choral, but in Part II, a setting of the Te Deum in Latin, the work also requires a very large double choir that is often divided into four separate choirs, and another chorus of boys' voices. There are four solo singers required as well, and in this second part Brian incorporates into his score four brass bands, placed in the four corners of the auditorium in the manner of Berlioz's Requiem. No wonder the score took eight years to complete, and to accommodate his vision Brian had to tape together 32-stave and 26-stave manuscript paper in order to produce a page of full score of 58 staves! What has often been remarked of this work is that despite the vast forces, Brian does not use them for one mind-blowing climax after another, but employs them with remarkable restraint and delicacy, reserving his fullest effects for the few moments that really demand them.

It is sometimes asked why Brian wrote the work for such gigantic forces. He must have known that the chances of ever hearing the work were almost non-existent, especially when written during the 1920s. A new generation of composers had arisen, and with them a new musical climate in complete contrast to the fashions prevalent prior to 1914; in a phrase the Gothic Symphony was superficially unfashionable. But on examining the score and hearing the work it becomes obvious that Brian's reason for choosing such forces was not some meretricious one – to write the largest symphony of all time – but so that the whole gamut of known instrumental colour at that time would be available to him to use as he wished. Brian may have used vast forces, as did Richard Strauss and Mahler, but his message was different from theirs: his polyphony stemmed from Byrd and the English madrigalists, not from his own contemporaries. Shortly after it was finished, Brian entered the work for the British section of the Schubert Centenary competition in 1928, the first prize of which was a cheque for £2,000 and a commercial recording. Apparently Brian only just missed the first prize, and it may well have been that the sheer cost of recording such a gigantic work led to his failure. However, the piece came to the attention of several distinguished musicians: Sir Donald Tovey regarded it as one of the greatest works by an Englishman, and Richard Strauss, who accepted the dedication, was enormously impressed by it. As is now tolerably well known, the work was not first performed until 1961 in a semi-amateur production in London. Its first fully professional performance was given in London in October 1966, conducted by Sir Adrian Boult. It might be asked why Brian did not make a greater effort to get his music performed – after all, with such a history already, by 1930 it would probably have been possible to get performances somewhere. But for Brian, always an indomitable man caring nothing for personal success, it was important for him to write the music and not by any means so important for him to hear it.

A Passing Tribute

The Gothic Symphony was called No 2, as Brian had in 1907 written a Fantastic Symphony in three movements. However, by this time the Fantastic had been broken up into two separate works, and some movements had been lost. The Gothic is now No 1.

In 1930 Brian began work on another large symphony, this time purely instrumental. It is this which is being performed at Brighton in April, but largely by amateur performers [in the event, two performances were given by the Kensington Symphony Orchestra under Leslie Head in May – on the 19th at the Dome in Brighton, on the 20th at the Victoria Hall, Hanley]; although the prospect of hearing the 'battle scherzo' of this work with its 16 horns, two pianos and three timpani is certainly exciting, an examination of the score would suggest that probably only a fully professional performance will do it justice. The Third Symphony (written in 1932) is in a sense a sinfonia concertante, with the two pianos of the Second's scherzo being elevated almost to concerto standing throughout the work, requiring staggering virtuosity.

The Fourth Symphony, finished in 1934, is Brian's only fully choral symphony. Subtitled *Das Siegeslied*, it is a three-movement setting of a text drawn from Psalm 68. Brian at this time was much attracted by German culture, (hardly 'fashionable' for a British composer in the 1930s) and the setting is in German. The rise of Nazism led to a disenchantment with Germany, and his next Symphony, No 5, came in great contrast. It is a work in one movement scored for baritone solo and comparatively small orchestra, a setting of Lord Alfred Douglas's poem, *Wine of Summer.*

In 1926, Brian became assistant editor of *Musical Opinion* and became known as a music critic. His championing of modern composers such as Berg and Schoenberg hardly endeared him to the musical establishment in England at that time. Another work written at about the same time as the *Wine of Summer* Symphony is his Violin Concerto which again suffered from the extraordinary series of misfortunes which dogged this man. The score was lost in London and when it became obvious that it would not be returned, Brian wrote another violin concerto, calling it No 2 but utilising themes used in the first. Shortly after this he began a work which in its demands far exceeds the performers required even for the Gothic. This was a vast, four-hour setting of Shelley's *Prometheus Unbound* and occupied Brian for nearly seven years, being completed in 1944. The score of this work has also disappeared.

At that time Brian was nearing 70, and must have felt that his life's work as a composer was coming to an end with this overwhelming composition, but in 1947 he wrote two symphonies in quick succession, the Sixth, *Sinfonia Tragica*, and the Seventh. These two works marked the transition to Brian's last phase as a composer, a phase so extraordinary that in contemplating his output after this time, one is reduced almost to a level of disbelief.

Between 1949 and 1968, between the ages of 73 and 92, he wrote, among many other works, 24 symphonies! This would be a remarkable achievement even if the music were worthless, but the more one comes to know of the works of this last period of Brian's life (and only four of the last 20 have been performed: 14, 18, 21, 22), the more one becomes convinced that in a sense, everything he wrote up to the end of the last war was a prelude to this astonishing final outpouring.

Brian often wrote works in groups. The Second, Third and Fourth Symphonies form a clear group, as do the Eighth, Ninth and Tenth. The Eighth dates from 1949, the Ninth from 1951 and the

A Passing Tribute

Tenth from 1954. It was in 1954 that Brian heard for the first time (at the age of 78!) any of his symphonies when Sir Adrian Boult conducted a broadcast performance of the Eighth. Possibly hearing his work was the spur for Brian's next symphony, No 11, very different from the preceding three, more intimate and contemplative, by no means as turbulent and tragic. All of the symphonies in Brian's last period are scored for a normal large orchestra, with none of the demands on instrumental resource that make the prospect of performance of the earlier symphonies so daunting. They rarely last for more than 25 minutes and some are in one movement. One of the most remarkable of these works is the Twelfth, written in 1957, lasting only twelve minutes yet containing a range of expression that is as wide as it is profound. I believe this work may well come to be recognised as one of Brian's greatest symphonies, in spite of its brevity.

It was around 1957 that I first came into contact with Havergal Brian in any meaningful sense when I attended the first performance of No 10 by the Philharmonia Orchestra under Stanley Pope at BBC's Maida Vale studios; I well remember my own astonishment at encountering such a major musical force. That the Tenth Symphony is a great masterpiece, I have no doubt; in the course of its 20-odd minutes, one feels that one has been listening to a work twice that length, simply because Brian packs so much musical incident into each moment that one is astonished that so much can be said in so short a space of time. The opening of the work, a tragic funeral march, is immediately arresting, and the succeeding first half, during which it seems as though a storm blows through the orchestra, aided by a vast percussion section containing wind and thunder machines, is one of the most remarkable passages in all music. Nor is this mere sensationalism: one has a feeling that one is being confronted by a living thing as though witnessing an extraordinary event of nature.

By the late 1950s, then, although Brian had written a large body of symphonies (twelve) he had not shown such a prolific creativity as he was soon to develop. It was around this time that Brian began to receive more attention than at any other period of his life, largely due to the efforts of Robert Simpson, and it may have been the occasional hearing of his symphonies as well as the interest shown in them that spurred his creative impulse. Between the end of 1959 and the end of 1960 he had written another five symphonies. Of these I have only heard No 14, a granite-like, violent work of immense power and strength.

By 1968 Brian had completed his cycle of thirty-two symphonies, but he also wrote during these years a Concerto for Orchestra, a comedy overture and a Cello Concerto. It has been said that if this story were told as fiction, it would be unbelievable. But it is true. A great many of these symphonies, as I write, have never been performed, so neither I nor the vast majority of people are in a position to judge them. It may be that in some of these later works Brian retraces his steps, but I think it is unlikely. What cannot be denied is that we will never know whether these later works are good, bad or indifferent until we have had a chance to hear them. No-one would be so foolish as to pretend that every new work that is performed is a masterpiece, but of the symphonies of Brian that I have heard (the Gothic, 8, 9, 10, 11, 12, 14, 18, 21 and 22), although I may rate some more highly than others, I have never been less than profoundly impressed.

On a personal level, what impressed me, on the occasions I

A Passing Tribute

visited him, apart from his indomitable energy and courage, was his personality. Although suffering decades of neglect he was entirely without bitterness or cynicism, with a lively interest in all forms of new music. For him, to get the music written was of paramount importance: like Beethoven, he was unable to hear his later music in performance, but it is not true, as some critics have maintained, that this lack of hearing his own music led him to make miscalculations. Before the astonishing outpouring of his last decade he had heard five of his later symphonies, and, although performances of his music were also infrequent before the last war, he had heard sufficient of his own works in later life to know what he was doing, to say nothing of his profound knowledge of other's music.

He is a composer of our time (indeed, passages of the third symphony – 1931! – rival Stockhausen in their instrumental layout and rhythmic complexity), and his later works could have been written at no other time than the post-Second World War era. But what sets him apart from his contemporaries is his profound humanity: his music is never cerebral, never pattern-making, and nothing seems to be calculated for 'effectiveness' – it is all put at the service of a truly original expression, entirely without external influence, yet with universal relevance.

At present, then, his music is known only to a small number of people, which begs the almost inevitable question of 'special pleading'. It is exciting news, therefore, that the BBC is to broadcast the complete 32 symphonies over the next three to four years, and comforting to know that Brian was aware of these plans shortly before he died. It gives all of us the chance to come to grips with this remarkable composer. Only time will tell, of course, but we owe it to ourselves to explore a composer unknown for far too long."

Chapter VI
Later Plans

When my article on Brian appeared in February, 1973 Mike Thorne appended an editorial note: "Havergal Brian's Symphonies Nos 10 and 21 were recorded by Angus McKenzie for Unicorn Records last summer, with Robert Simpson producing, and Eric Pinkett and James Loughran conducting the Leicestershire Schools Symphony Orchestra." The disc was eventually issued in May, 1973 when it created, as indeed it deserved to, something of an impact. This was a real breakthrough, and the previous month Lyrita had taped the Tragica and the Sixteenth (which, in the case of the latter work, as we have seen, waited until 1994 for its first public performance), although two years elapsed before Lyrita actually issued their recording.

Nonetheless, things did appear to be happening on the record front with regard to Brian's music, and several months after my article had appeared, Leonard Bernstein returned for a Stravinsky concert and stayed at the Savoy. This time, I visited him at his suite, taking with me the score of the 'Gothic'. Bernstein had certainly heard of Brian and of the work, through – I think – my colleague, Paul Myers, who was of course aware of my keenness for Brian's music. Bernstein spent about two hours studying the music in detail, humming a little and saying, "God, that's ----ing difficult!" at

77

HAVERGAL BRIAN

certain passages, but was thrilled at the closing pages of the Scherzo. When he had finished, he looked up and said, "Bob, I'd love to do the 'Gothic' but you know that my life is planned in detail for the next five years or so. If you can persuade Edinburgh or Salzburg or Vienna to want it, then I'll do it." I knew that would guarantee a recording and a film – this was before the arrival of 'videos' as such.

Coincidentally, that tireless champion of the unusual in music, Edward Johnson, had sent Bernstein a score of the 'Gothic'; in a note of thanks, the conductor wrote of the music as "overwhelming".

A few days later, I found myself sitting next to the fine Hungarian-born musician Laszlo Heltay at dinner in Claridges and we spoke at some length about choral works, including Brian's *Psalm 23* which Heltay had conducted at that year's Brighton Festival. Neither of us knew that we should soon collaborate on a Brian recording. Outsiders should know that a person holding the job I had did not have a limitless supply of money for recording projects, and that the cost of a recording by a major artist, if not originated in New York, would have to be borne by the originating company. Most of the UK's recording budget was taken up by already-committed plans for John Williams and Pierre Boulez (both signed initially to the UK Company). I knew it would have been a waste of time talking to Boulez about Brian and what I also then knew was that Bernstein's long-cherished plan to record Bizet's 'Carmen' had been turned down by CBS's New York office – and had been taken up by DGG, who were 'after' Bernstein. In spite of Bernstein's encouragement I knew that any idea of his doing the 'Gothic' would meet with incomprehension by DGG, and very soon after then any decision about a CBS recording of

Later Plans

Brian's music by a major international artist was largely taken out of my immediate hands by my promotion to Director of Marketing at the company. This meant that I was now in charge of pop, jazz, folk, rock, shows, classical, promotion, marketing, advertising, artist liaison in all of these fields, sleeve design, press and publicity, through a vast army of staff who reported directly to me.

This was a hot seat, yet I did not forget my old friend and when the chance came to make a recording of three of Brian's works with the Leicestershire Schools Symphony Orchestra I took it like a shot. It may seem strange that on the one hand I was advocating fully-professional performances and recordings of Brian's music – much of his demanding later music had been given by well-meaning amateurs, who were, frankly, not up to the task – and on the other I embraced a Schools Orchestra recording of this very music.

Brian was in my opinion an utter original, a composer whose late-period symphonies are written in a language which is modern, difficult to comprehend at a first hearing, and which would stretch intellectually and technically the powers of the world's greatest conductors and orchestras. How could one urge fully professional performances by great artists and accept the Leicestershire Schools Symphony Orchestra? The answer was that this orchestra had already recorded Brian's Tenth and Twenty-first Symphonies for Unicorn and had done an outstanding job; a professional recording is not the same as a live performance: passages can be worked on again and again, editing can make a continuous performance free from the inevitable slips and errors that bedevil live amateur orchestral playing, and the enthusiasm of this particular body would, I thought, carry all before it. Quite apart from anything else, the cost involved was very reasonable, and enjoying the position I held, I could direct the release of this album personally. I had decided that the release should be at mid-price, making Brian's music available to a wider public, and the record would form part of a series of mid-price albums of British music: I had already issued the Beecham album of music by Arnell and Berners and a valuable coupling of Vaughan Williams's Fourth & Sixth Symphonies and had several others planned. In addition, the Leicestershire album could lead to more. Finally, the music chosen was only representative in small part – the Symphony No 22 – of Brian's late style; it included his early setting of *Psalm 23*, his first extant choral work, with Laszlo Heltay conducting, and the *Fifth English Suite*.

Eric Pinkett and, I think, William Robson came to see me at my office in Theobald's Road, together with the talented young man I had appointed to succeed me in my classical job, David Rossiter – who was later to found Et Cetera Records before tragically dying from a brain tumour. I knew that David was not a Brian 'nut' but he saw the advantage for CBS of the plan I had set in train and was an enthusiastic supporter of the idea. I looked through the score of the *Fifth English Suite* with these gentlemen and I think they were rather taken aback when I pointed out a mistake in the first bar of the brass in the last movement, after a cursory glance: it leaped from the page at me. Their surprise was that all around us were the sounds of Abba, The Three Degrees, Mott the Hoople and so on, and a lively bustling crowd of fashionably dressed young men and women keen to promote the latest rock album – all of the exciting things that make up the marketing department of a successful international record company – and yet here I was, the boss of these people, pointing out an error in a Havergal Brian manuscript!

Later Plans

Knowing that Robert Simpson himself would be in charge of the sessions, and, with Mike Thorne's encouragement, Angus McKenzie the recording engineer, I decided that my presence would be unnecessary. Laszlo Heltay was also to conduct Brian's Twenty-second Symphony as well as the setting, dating originally from 1901, of *Psalm 23*. I assumed that all would go well but I learned that there were some last-minute hitches – indeed, an indication of these only became clear to me when reading of them in Lewis Foreman's book *Havergal Brian and the performance of his orchestral music*, though I should think they may have been exaggerated – but not by Foreman. What cannot be disputed is that Laszlo Heltay got better results than did Eric Pinkett in the Suite, which was recorded in Leicester without Robert Simpson producing. I am not pointing a finger at anyone, certainly not after this length of time, but it may well have been that the Suite posed more problems for the orchestra than any of us thought it would. I should perhaps mention Lewis Foreman's book: when it appeared, I was asked to review it for *Classical Music* and I was critical of it. Looking back on it now, I can appreciate the effort and hard work which it must have cost the author and my strictures then were expressed more forcibly than if I were asked to comment on it today.

However, I was quite happy with the finished tape, and had spoken with another Hungarian, Roslav Szaybo, who was my art director at CBS; we had chosen an existing American cover for the Brian, and the album was at last issued at the beginning of 1975, just at the point where I had left CBS to join RCA. I had done a good job at CBS, I think, and one of my legacies was a Classical Dealer Scheme, whereby dealers all over the country undertook to sign up to one of three systems which guaranteed delivery to them of a certain number of copies of every classical album, with full exchangeability rights and an additional discount on all of their classical business. This meant that every CBS classical record, including the Havergal Brian album, was in every shop that sold classical LPs in Britain in the first week of release.

In the first week alone, it shipped and sold over 1,700 copies. I felt that this was an excellent start, but I was, within days, with a rival company. A month later, Ray Burford – who remained at CBS to do an outstanding job – told me that sales of the Brian disc had exceeded 2,000 copies. I much regret that CBS did not follow up the connexion with the Leicestershire Schools Orchestra to make a series of Havergal Brian albums – the orchestra had other Brian scores, and, with proper production methods and adequate recording time – as the Unicorn album had shown – even better results could have been obtained.

At RCA, I had a very different job; although I was in charge of the UK Classical Department this – like CBS – relied very much at first on new recordings coming from the USA. Having launched James Galway's career in 1975, employing many pop marketing techniques I had used at CBS, I had a greater freedom and was encouraged in this by a succession of Managing Directors; after all, to have had, as I did, three classical albums in the UK Top 50 pop album charts in the same week, without tv advertising, was not to be sneezed at. It had not happened before, and has not been equalled since. In this, I was helped by my promotions administrator, Madeleine Kasket, whom I had brought into the music business from EMI Television Productions. One of the artists I had personally signed to RCA was the Iranian conductor and composer Loris Tjeknavorian. I had much faith in his ability as a conductor, and

82

Later Plans

learned that he was, being of Armenian extraction, a Christian working within the Islamic world. Loris had been appointed Court Composer to the Shah of Iran and I was presented to the Shah's wife, Empress Farah, during a visit she made to England. Her Majesty also admired Loris Tjeknavorian, and I told her of several large-scale plans involving him which I hoped would come to fruition. One of these projects, set up by RCA's Managing Director, the mercurial Dutchman, Gerry Oord, was for Loris to record with the Leningrad Philharmonic in Russia; another was for Loris to perform the 'Gothic' in London and in Leningrad and to record it. The Empress told me that she would endeavour to be present at the London performance of the 'Gothic' if it could be arranged.

I had shown Loris Tjeknavorian the score of the 'Gothic' and had played him a tape of Boult's 1966 performance at my home. He had heard of Havergal Brian through his friend, Ateş Orga, who had also written on Brian some years before, and I was keen to see what RCA's great record producer Charles Gerhardt and his gifted colleague George Korngold (the son of Erich Wolfgang Korngold) would make of this extraordinary score at London's Kingsway Hall, with Kenneth Wilkinson as recording engineer. Loris was keen to do the 'Gothic' but I knew it would take several years before it could be achieved. During that time, a fundamentalist Islamic revolution was set in train in Iran, forcing the Shah and his family to seek exile abroad, and placing at some personal risk those who had been connected with the Court. Amongst those who suffered in this way was Loris Tjeknavorian. A musician who had been admired by his country's rulers, this quiet, gentle man found himself cut off from his home and members of his family, forced to travel from country to country on temporary permits, until, after many vicissitudes, he was able to make a new home and career for himself in his native Armenia. All plans for 'Gothic' performances and a recording of it by him were abandoned.

However, before these events, to commemorate the Silver Jubilee of Queen Elizabeth II in 1977, I planned a series of albums of British music. One of them came about through a neighbour, Leslie Lake, a guiding light of the fine Locke Brass Consort as well as being bass trombonist of the Orchestra of the English National Opera. I had wanted to produce an album of British fanfares, and here was the opportunity; we had a lot of fun planning this record at my home which was recorded in Morden under the talented conductor, James Stobart. I was the record producer and I also contributed the unsigned liner notes. Leslie Lake and I incorporated Brian's *Festival Fanfare* of 1967 alongside Robert Simpson's *Canzona for Brass*, and we included music by Edmund Rubbra (one of 11 works by this composer I was to record and issue during my time at RCA) and Leslie's own reconstruction of Elgar's *Civic Fanfare*. Although this was, in the nature of things, a minor contribution to the Brian canon, the final combination on the one record of music by my two old friends gave me the greatest personal satisfaction.

Recordings mentioned in Chapter VI

CBS

HAVERGAL BRIAN
Symphony No 22 'Symphonia Brevis' (1965) 9:03
Leicestershire Schools Symphony Orchestra
conducted by Laszlo Heltay

Psalm XXIII – for tenor, chorus and orchestra (1901) 15:41
Paul Taylor, tenor; Brighton Festival Chorus
Leicestershire Schools Symphony Orchestra
conducted by Laszlo Heltay

English Suite No 5 'Rustic Scenes' (1953) 22:41
Leicestershire Schools Symphony Orchestra
conducted by Eric Pinkett

CBS Classics 61612

Producers: Robert Simpson (Symphony and Psalm 23), William
    Robson (English Suite)
Recording Engineer: Angus McKenzie
Recording Venues: Hove Town Hall (Symphony and Psalm 23)
    De Montfort Hall, Leicester (English Suite)
Recorded: 1974
Album Co-Ordinator: Robert [Matthew-]Walker, CBS Records
Released: February, 1975

RCA

Jubilant Brass – British Music for Symphonic Brass Ensemble

HAVERGAL BRIAN:
Festival Fanfare: Fanfare for the Orchestral Brass (1967) 1:45

ROBERT SIMPSON:
Canzona for Brass (1958)   5:22

with Music by: Benjamin, Bliss, Elgar, Jacob,
Rubbra, Tippett, Walton.

The Locke Brass Consort conducted by James Stobart

RCA Red Seal RL 25081 (LP) RK 25081 (MC)

Producer: Robert Matthew-Walker
Recording Engineer: Brian Couzens
Recording Venue: St Peter's Church, Morden, Surrey
Recorded: February 20 & 21, 1977
Released: June, 1977
Reissued: Chandos CHAN 6573 (CD) Fanfares

Chapter VII
A Redeemed Artist

"He who forever strives with all his might
That man we can redeem."
"These words, chanted by the angels in Goethe's Faust, are prefixed as a motto to Havergal Brian's Gothic Symphony; they could stand as a motto for his whole life." Indeed they could. With this quotation, Deryck Cooke began his programme note for the 1966 Boult performance of this Symphony, when the composer was still alive and when his presence at a performance of his music would guarantee spontaneous and affectionate applause over and above that which the work itself might generate.

The story of Brian's life is truly, as Robert Simpson pointed out in 1958, "an extraordinary one, almost without parallel", yet the life of an artist, no matter how it has been led, or what happens to him during it, is of little significance in considering the art itself: for those of us who are left and those who come after, the importance is what this art means to us, today, and, in its relevant reinterpretation, to future generations. We, ourselves, form part of such 'future generations', for it will soon be a quarter of a century since Brian's death, thirty years after his long life's work came to an end.

There are those who feel that future generations should take care of themselves – as, indeed, those of us who are loving parents hope they will – and we should not bother too much about them. Yet this cannot mean, in terms of basic humanity, that what we do should be without what Elgar referred to in discussing his First Symphony (a work that Havergal Brian deeply admired) as "a massive hope for the future". Man can be stupid, yes – as we have seen all too often in the twentieth century – but he can be wise, also, and if art has any meaning at all, any generic sense of purpose, it is to enhance our lives, to make our lives better.

A farm labourer in Italy in the sixteenth century may have been illiterate in today's terms but every Sunday, at Mass, he would worship in a church wherein he would hear noble music, see great architecture and paintings, and – if he were lucky – hear, through biblical readings and sermons, fine language spoken and moral precepts enunciated. He would experience these things alongside members of every stratum of society; they would all, poet and peasant, prelate and prince, be touched by the finer manifestations of European culture, whether they believed in an after-life or not, or whether they 'understood' this culture or not.

Today, it is not the Mass, but the Mass-media, which unites people throughout the world: we have to cope with the all-pervasive medium of television, wherein subjects lacking a strong visual element are either not broadcast at all, or, if they happen to be, are done so in ways which can be positively harmful. We are in danger, perhaps, of thereby losing contact with great art which does not have a visual element – literature, poetry, concert music – and even that art which possesses a visual element – drama, painting, sculpture, ballet and opera – is often treated by television in ways that neither respect nor illuminate the subject. Football matches,

A Redeemed Artist

throughout the world, are 'analysed' by experts on television, after the games have been played, in ways that should convince even an ardent sporting sceptic that there may be some merit in the game after all, and yet the broadcast of a symphony or string quartet will nowadays often take place only in terms of 'visual' presentation – pictures of the composer, his home, a country house or an opera house's internal decor, for examples – without any 'analysis' whatsoever. In the mid 1950s, Leonard Bernstein, on prime time American television, was able to speak of Beethoven's Fifth Symphony in a way which had New York cab drivers the following morning asking their fares if they had seen his fascinating programme. It can be done – all it needs is broadcasters of genuine vision, breadth of artistic sympathy, intelligence and a feeling for the televisual medium.

The way in which society's media covers the arts in general should give us cause for alarm. Too often, it appears, art is treated by the media as if it were a branch of entertainment. Art can, of course, be 'entertaining', but that is not the same thing. More corrosively, it seems, the reverse is gaining ground. 'Entertainment' is treated as if it were on the same level as art: in other words, that both are things people might wish to give their attention to in their free time. 'Entertainment' – comedy, popular music, popular 'culture' – can possess artistic merit, but not all of it does. The result of equating popular entertainment with art is the trivialisation of art, especially great art, treating it as some fashionable adjunct to our lives and not showing it to be an imperishable thing in itself (so long as we permit human life to remain imperishable), the study of which can enhance our lives by bringing us into contact with the finest manifestations of the human spirit expressed in transcendental terms. Such manifestations – which clearly are not to be found in television game shows or sitcoms – were often achieved only after a lifetime of striving by the lone artist.

So if the music of Havergal Brian – alongside that of many another composer – in our society is, on the one hand, in real danger of becoming further sidelined through the way in which art in general is disseminated today, we can take comfort from the fact that on the other hand the worldwide availability in due course of his symphonies on compact disc is the best possible news. His music demands, as indeed does all music, professional and deeply committed performances from artists who believe in it. It then deserves to be written about by those who have a grasp of the music itself, in ways that convince the unprejudiced reader. To judge by the initial results, the first requirement is, largely, what it will receive. The advantages of records are manifold: we can study the music and get to know it well at our own pace, and it may be that the existence of one or other recording of a Brian symphony will inspire conductors elsewhere to perform his music.

In these ways, and by whatever other means are used, there can be no doubt that Brian's music will come to be seen worthy of reinterpretation and appreciated as great art.

When a musician, or a group of musicians, is convinced that the work of a composer constitutes great art – especially a composer whose music is hardly known – he can either keep his views to himself or tell others about it. In 1949 Harold Truscott knew that Brian was a great composer, and his advocacy in a now-defunct music journal struck the writer of these words in a way which contributed to his own personal appreciation of Brian's greatness. After many years of studying and thinking about this music, I do

A Redeemed Artist

not now agree with everything Truscott wrote of Brian's work, or indeed with everything other musicians have written. Even at this level, such 'reinterpretation' is not only possible, but desirable. Like all great music Brian's can bear wide interpretation in performance and if I hear the 'Gothic' differently in some ways from Harold Truscott or from Malcolm MacDonald and others, and because I believe that this symphony, more than any other composition of Brian's, lies at the heart of his life's work, then for the sake of what value they may be to other listeners, present or future, I append below some observations on the 'Gothic', principally on the first three movements, and on what I perceive to be part of Brian's compositional processes in them which to my knowledge have not been remarked upon before. What follows is not, of course, an 'analysis' in the generally-accepted sense; the work demands a book to itself. These observations have enhanced my sense of wonder and fulfilment on hearing this symphony after more than 20 years' study of it, and may go towards answering criticism sometimes levelled against the work, even by Brian admirers. In this way, these observations ought perhaps to be considered as appendices to the admirable essays on the 'Gothic' by Harold Truscott and Paul Rapoport [published by the Havergal Brian Society in one volume, 1978] and that by Malcolm MacDonald [Vol I of his three-volume study of the Brian Symphonies, published by Kahn and Averill, 1974]. My comments on the work do not take into account the enormous emotional content and power of this music, which of course will affect each listener differently to some degree, but which cannot be divorced from whatever technical means are employed to express Brian's astounding vision.

The 'Gothic' Symphony, for all its length – about an hour and

91

three quarters – is, from the very beginning, a continuous work which, for its proper impact to be felt, has to be experienced as a continuous, truly unbroken process, a point well made by Malcolm MacDonald and by Harold Truscott. When I write "truly unbroken" I do not overlook the natural pauses in the music in the second part, the setting of the 'Te Deum'; they are no more than the music demands, in much the same way as the pauses in a movement by Bruckner are dictated by the inherent nature of the music itself. The end of the first movement of the 'Gothic' is marked *attacca* – that is, follow immediately with the next music, the second movement, which in turn is inextricably linked to the Scherzo by a bass clarinet solo; the Scherzo leads completely without a break to the 'Te Deum'. No matter how vast this conception is, as Harold Truscott has pointed out, an hour and three quarters is not an excessive amount of unbroken time for an audience to see a film or to hear an act in a Wagner opera; why should it be considered too much for a symphony in concert? Mahler's Third Symphony approaches the 'Gothic' in terms of length, and that work is nowadays rarely given with an interval; therefore, for its fullest appreciation, the 'Gothic' must be heard continuously. When that happens, Brian's deepest original processes in the work – different from those of any other composer – are more likely to become clearer.

What are these processes, and how are they achieved? Let us step back a little from the 'Gothic' and consider for a moment Brian as an artist. The reader may have heard the phrase 'a great and true original' – but what does this mean? In what way was Brian 'original' when some commentators, not all of them musically incompetent, regarded him as a pale reflection of earlier masters?

Those whose music Brian is said palely to reflect are turn-of-

A Redeemed Artist

the-century masters, in particular Richard Strauss, whom it is known Brian admired. The fashion for what was termed *Empfindsamkeit* – sensibility or sensitivity – led to the widespread Romantic movement in nineteenth-century music, the greatest masters being Berlioz, Schumann, Liszt, Wagner and (somewhat later) Tchaikovsky. Later still, the leading late-Romantic masters were Mahler and Richard Strauss. By the beginning of the twenti-eth-century an anti-Romantic movement in the arts had begun. This anti-Romanticism saw music lagging behind other arts, but the reaction against a largely all-pervasive style was fraught with uncertainty, as weaker creative characters adopted Romanticism as a norm whilst stronger individuals rejected it at their peril. The pervasive 'style' was in danger of becoming inherently schismatic: such superficial elements of sentimentality and self-projection – the results of exaggerating the *empfindsamkeit* characteristics to the detriment of structural unity – became incompatible with the classical principle of tonality on which the Romantic movement in music had been founded.

The evolution of this classical principle, in the Romantic era, was weakened, as was so often the case, as a result of misunderstand-ing aspects of Beethoven's late music. His final masterpieces – the Ninth Symphony, *Missa Solemnis*, 'Hammerklavier' Sonata, the first version of opus 130, the 'Diabelli' Variations – are on a large scale, and this element of size, in itself, was superficially taken by many Romantic composers as *de rigeur* – many, it appeared, had to begin their careers with large-scale works. Beethoven's sense of size, of scale, or – better still, in Harold Truscott's 1949 phrase – his sense of proportion in these works was something he had evolved for himself, a result in large measure of his realisation of the creative

HAVERGAL BRIAN

dynamic set free by the juxtaposition in his work of tonalities, or keys, a third apart, arising from the tonic and dominant of key-relationships and coincidentally, through such juxtaposition, creating an additional redefinition of major and minor modes. This juxtaposition fuels much of Beethoven's work from his 'Eroica' Symphony onwards.

This basis of keys a third apart informs almost all music of the Romantic movement, and which, stretched almost to breaking-point through the fixed major-minor convention, ultimately led to a collapse of classical tonality in the late 1890s and early 1900s. Not all composers during this period were 'Romantics' in this sense: Bruckner was not, neither was Brahms, nor Dvořák, amongst others. In turn, it was the superficial elements of the Romanticism of such great and original masters as Liszt, Berlioz and Wagner — including the employment of large orchestras and the dramatic gesture — which were adopted by composers as rules, without understanding what it was that lay at the heart of their music — a strong tonal basis — even if, in the case of these three masters in particular, the expansion of tonality through the growth of chromaticism and (somewhat less influential) a greater tonal freedom in the relationship of certain keys to the tonic in the music of Liszt and, later, Wagner, together with Berlioz's original use of the *idée fixe*, or, later still, the French cyclical development of the 'motto' theme; all of these individual factors stretched classical principles.

Some later composers, also large-scale thinkers, reverted to tonal principles without exhibiting the exaggerated characteristics of late-Romanticism. Amongst these were the Scandinavians Sibelius and Nielsen, both original in their use of structure and tonality; another was Bartók who rewrote his own musical language

A Redeemed Artist

from first principles (after early fascination with late-Romanticism) but whose creation of large-scale works was based not upon tonal principles, but upon additive, vibrative, thematic cellular derivation and the relegation of tonal elements to a subsidiary role. In Bartók's case, his originality led his admirers and imitators to claim, for example, that his string quartets were the heirs of those by Beethoven: as Bartók's quartets were written from an utterly different set of compositional principles – in which tonality assumed a secondary function – nothing could be further from the musical truth.

Schoenberg evolved another technical solution, even though he was temperamentally an arch-Romantic, and so did Hindemith, as also, to a lesser technical degree, did Stravinsky through the sheer force of his creative personality – creative 'time-travelling', as it was called, as he sought revivifying elements from earlier periods. An older master, Debussy, found revivification from fresh scales and, from Berlioz, the structural functions of texture (not unallied to Debussy's rarely-appreciated mastery of counterpoint). Others took a similar route to Bartók's: folk music, as exemplified in masters as different as Vaughan Williams and Copland, who, like others still, also turned to recent 'non-classical' developments: jazz, popular elements, and – in Milhaud's case – the use of bitonality (a frequently misunderstood subject) which reached its zenith in the third of his Cinq Etudes for piano and orchestra: four fugues heard simultaneously in different keys.

These solutions in all their variety and different degrees of success arose from the problem faced by all composers at some point: is the existing language of music suitable for their needs? Is it possible – or even desirable – to create a new way of saying what has to be said entirely from scratch, or can one use the existing language in a new and re-creative manner? The creation of new musical languages in the early twentieth century was the result of reactions against late-Romanticism, yet, at a practical, if mundane, level, these results led millions of music-lovers to complain about the unintelligibility of so much modern music, without bothering to learn the new languages in order to understand just what it was that these composers were trying to express.

Classical tonal principles demanded that music should be in a key: no matter which but the key in which a work began would be the same as that at which the music's ending would naturally be expected to arrive. There are always exceptions, especially amongst works of genius: Mendelssohn's 'Italian' Symphony is in A major, but its brilliant *Saltarello* finale is in A minor, anticipated more than thirty years earlier in Jan Dussek's E major Piano Sonata, Opus 10, No 3 – the finale is in E minor. Chopin's Fantasy, Opus 49 in F minor ends, convincingly, in A flat major: this can be cited as an early type of 'progressive tonality' (the evolution of one tonality from another), yet both keys are strongly related. In any case, there is an earlier Fantasy – Beethoven's (of course) in G minor, Opus 77, which ends astoundingly in B major. Nor has this elliptical masterpiece ever been adequately analysed.

Havergal Brian was 25 years old when Queen Victoria died in 1901, the year of his first extant choral work, *Psalm 23*, and the language, if not always the aesthetic, of late-Romanticism came most naturally to him. He had no need for a new musical language, for, apart from anything else, Brian was a working-class 'outsider' who sought to belong; his artistic psychology demanded that he spoke a similar language to those he aspired to join. Brian's earlier music shows him grappling with the problem, already striking out individually, as in his setting of *Psalm 23*, and in the 'Gothic' he solved it from within the existing language. He did this by rejecting the Romantic keys-a-third-apart convention and by making one key evolve from another – not a third apart. The result is a dynamic inter-action of tonality, quite natural in itself, which can, of course, support large-scale structures whilst being unlike anything else in twentieth-century music. Or almost. The 'Gothic' traverses a tonal journey in which one key, E major, evolves from that next to it, D. Brian was not the only composer to have looked at tonality from such a different viewpoint, nor is what happens in the 'Gothic' necessarily always akin to what has been termed 'progressive tonality' (a term which can be misleading; it has sometimes thus been used in discussions of Robert Simpson's music, and of the music of another composer whom Simpson did much to champion, Carl Nielsen) yet Brian's new way of using tonality and keys provided a natural, dynamic and original basis for his music which springs fully-formed, for the first time, in the 'Gothic'.

The 'Gothic's' magnificent, entirely characteristic, opening is in a trenchant D minor in which the interval of the minor third D-F is all-important. The note F defines the minor mode exactly, in a way which a bare fifth D-A does not; the mood is eruptively severe, the more so as the timpanists ram home the two notes D-F. We know, because we have heard the music, and read about it before, that the ultimate goal of the Symphony, in tonal terms, is E major, a rise of one whole tone. E is between D and F, and is here trapped by these notes, as a pincer at the outset. To be equidistant, the F should be raised, to F sharp, making one whole tone either side of E.

Almost as soon as the work has begun, the harps pull back a curtain to reveal an entirely different vista: an "almost too beautiful" (as Malcolm MacDonald rightly says) landscape, a 'second subject' in D flat major – so near and yet so far in many ways. This is a false dawn, for the tonality has slipped so early on, not risen, on its journey towards E. With these two main ideas, Brian has mapped out a truly immense canvas; as MacDonald again rightly points out, Brian's later habit of sudden juxtapositions was in his symphonies literally from the start, but this is not a typical sonata structure, such as the use of 'first and second subjects' implies, at all: how could it be, for we know that within the hour we shall be hearing a setting of the 'Te Deum' and is there a 'typical sonata structure' in genuinely late-Romantic music? We cannot criticise Brian for not being what we expect him to be.

This first movement is fully integral to the work in setting out the parameters of the whole conception. I tend to agree with Harold Truscott that the true tonality of the second subject is not D flat but D major, which key arrives a few bars later, and that the slide into D flat is necessary to avoid any tonal similarity between first and second subjects – Chopin, again, may be recalled, in his E minor Concerto, wherein the first movement's second subject appears initially in the tonic major, and in the first movement of his Piano Trio in G minor, as Leslie Howard has pointed out, the second subject also appears at first in the tonic. Brian's avoidance of close tonal similarity between first and second subjects forms part of the 'Gothic's' tonal destination: the second subject in an extreme flat-key in this Symphony immediately rises – cancelling out the semitonal fall – and by so doing reveals a new and different aspect to the opening D minor, edging the overall tonal scheme of this first

A Redeemed Artist

movement towards D major.

E major cannot, therefore, evolve from the first subject in D minor, but can through the second subject in D major. The opening movement, therefore, has to strive to assert D major, for two main reasons: the first is to establish the F-sharp mediant, making E equidistant between the notes that define D major, and the second is that D major, being a sharp key, is closer to E major than to D minor. Once D major has been established, the goal of E major is nearer. Another reason for this movement not being composed along traditional tonal lines is that, if it were, the ending would at least imply a return to the opening D minor region from which Brian wishes the music to be set free.

And so the movement proceeds to its remarkable conclusion, reinforced by a new sound – that of full organ. This new timbre in the symphony may to some listeners bring with it the connotation of a cathedral, and with that, of choral singing. This dramatic instrumental gesture is, more importantly, part of the musical fabric, for it quite literally brings another element to bear on the establishment, however momentary in the long run, of D major. It is as though the new timbre startles us into taking this event very seriously.

This movement has been criticised for spending too much time, through a relaxation of the basic pulse, on the second subject. But this second subject is, of its nature, more melodic, and it therefore expands – is developed – in those terms. It also provides the basis for the entire symphony's themes, at the same time as being derived from what should be recognised as the germ of the whole work – the opening interval of a third. The second subject opens with the inversion of the rising third interval – a falling sixth

HAVERGAL BRIAN

from F natural (now the third in a pentatonic scale on D flat) – and expands therefrom.

The music, having slid momentarily flatwards so to speak, uses the material positively towards its goal: as C sharp, D flat takes on new aspects; it is both the leading note of D major, and as a key in itself is also the relative minor of E major, which latter key momentarily now appears before us as the movement heads towards its end. This almost immediately becomes E minor, wherein both G natural and D natural are better placed to assist in the establishment of D major, which is done – astoundingly, contradicting 'traditional' harmony – without reference to the dominant, A, and with the enharmonic of D flat, C sharp minor acting as the preparatory tonality (as the tonic's leading note, and also as a chromatic chord) for the establishment of D. With such processes afoot, this movement cannot be thought of as the weakest in the work; it is surely fully up to the level of the others.

Immediately, the slow movement begins, on F sharp (of which C sharp is the dominant). This reinforces the major mediant of D, and, as a tonal region, rather than a tonality in itself, balances that of the first movement. We may observe that this 'balancing' is not of itself any answer at all, and, embracing the "almost too beautiful" theme from the first movement, this funereal march begins with a variant of the fourth bar of that second subject, the opening third now in the major. In mood, this is not unlike 'Saturn' from Holst's *The Planets*, but the F-sharp (changing to G flat, of which the dominant is D flat from the first movement's initial statement of its second subject – a further pointer to the long-term rejection of D, or, should one say, E double flat) at length falls a minor third to D sharp (E flat) minor, which is half-way between D and E. D minor

A Redeemed Artist

itself has also returned but has been thwarted by the same sideways slip, to a semitone below, that we heard in the first movement, and the music gradually moves upwards through E flat minor and E minor – as in the first movement – and up again to F sharp (avoiding F – D minor), from which note (as G flat) a bass clarinet winds downwards to link to the phantasmagorical Scherzo, in D minor to begin with. Such a bare (and necessarily incomplete) sketch-plan of aspects of the tonal outline of this slow movement in no way considers, or compensates for, the overwhelming emotional character of this music, which reaches in technical terms far forward, towards the end of the twentieth century and into the twenty-first. "Tremendously contemporary in feeling", wrote Sir Eugène Goossens to Brian after the first performance of the 'Gothic' [page 47], with particular reference to the Scherzo; in terms of relevance (and therefore contemporaneity), perhaps what Goossens said could be better expressed, more than thirty years later, by the music's 'timelessness' in feeling.

Why D minor for the Scherzo, after all that has gone before? Harold Truscott put his finger on it when he wrote of the extraordinary section towards the end of the Scherzo being "perhaps the crucial passage in the entire symphony". His likening this to a kind of symphonic "black hole", through which one passes unable to return, is spot on; the harmonic events in the Symphony's first two movements have created a strong sense of forward-movement, of a large living organism in time, not in space, but the implications of these events have not been fully explored. Nor are they to be here, but the vivid, fertile D minor which began the Symphony has never been entirely eliminated, even by the establishment of D major and also by that of its mediant, F sharp. It is as though a battle having been won, the war is still not over. The force which brought the Symphony to powerful life still has to be faced, or rather, put to more constructive use: D minor has to be revisited, albeit differently. Indeed, this revisitation is so different that the mediant F is not stated at all for 15 bars of the opening Brucknerian ostinato, with the result that when it is heard, as part of the oboe's first theme, the full establishment of D minor appears complete. 'Appears', (simply) because in the bass we have dimly been aware of a dislocating flattened sixth, B flat, which in the event pulls the tonality to F major-minor for what euphemistically has been termed the 'trio' theme, on horns, which is, thematically, a variant of the oboe theme and which had been anticipated in the first movement. The contrast is textural and tonal, not thematic, which, to note one small but not insignificant point, is established with the same third (minor this time) which thematically began the first two movements. This D minor is different: every time it appears, it is 'accompanied', or succeeded, by disruptive elements – rather ineffective at first and gradually becoming ever more fantastic and uneasy: fragments of themes from the first movement, recalled as if in a fevered dream and quite brilliantly and unnervingly scored, pass by, and as soon disappear. A reference to the 'trio' in F major – with an added sixth (D) in the bass now equally disruptive in itself – unleashes a veritable storm in which scraps of material from the first two movements fly by. Then, "the crucial passage in the entire symphony" is upon us. Words cannot adequately describe the effect this astounding music has either on the listener or on the progress of the work itself: here is the progenitor of the 'storm' in the Tenth Symphony which so gripped my teenage imagination; but the result is to swallow up the events of the Symphony until

A Redeemed Artist

now, leaving a dim memory of the 'trio', receding further and further from our perception, overtaken by something new, a D major chord with an added sixth – B, the dominant of E major, on fifth horn. In the alternative chord provided if the first three movements are performed separately the B is also to be found within the harps' quasi-pentatonic tracery.

Why has all of this happened harmonically in this manner? The answer surely lies in the relationship between D and F – the opening notes of the symphony, from which everything has germinated. The F in the Scherzo was so long delayed until, now as a key itself (nudged forward by the added sixth, B flat, whose dominant it also is) it utterly reinforces the seemingly ineradicable D minor.

In describing aspects of this music on the preceding page I wrote that "fragments of themes from the first movement . . . and . . . a reference to the 'trio' in F major . . . unleash . . . a veritable storm [leading to] 'the crucial passage in the entire symphony' ", quoting the last phrase from Harold Truscott. As the F major tonality of the 'trio' reinforces with considerable certainty the tonality of D minor, then we are back in the very region from which the music has expended so much effort in escaping; hence the "fragments of themes from the first movement". Nor are these events in the living organism of this symphony expressed in what might be termed a 'human' manner – it is as though we are witnesses to some frightening natural event. And the 'dehumanising' of the music at this point – the rejection of late-Romanticism's self-projection through a final tonal rejection of a classical key-system which, in Beethoven's hands led to the keys-a-third-apart syndrome (the keys-a-third-apart in this instance being D minor and F major) of the Romantic movement – brings us into direct confrontation with a new force, a new language of music almost, threatening to overthrow everything that has gone before, "leaving a dim memory of the 'trio', receding further and further from our perception, overtaken by something new, a D major chord with an added sixth – B, the dominant of E major . . ."

Boult did not play the added sixth B, and the Aries LP issue of his performance stupidly includes the 'wrong' chord – that which Brian wrote if only the first three movements were played separately; the chord that begins Part II proper, the 'Te Deum' is not the same in instrumentation, and naturally includes the added sixth B, which has a practical purpose as well as an essential tonal one: to enable the boys' and girls' chorus accurately to pitch their opening B. Now, the opening thirds, minor and major, which began each of the first three movements set this great second part of the work in motion, with a bitonal choral setting of the opening words of the Te Deum: boys and girls in B minor, sopranos and altos in D major: if this does not also demonstrate a logical necessity of playing the D major/added-sixth chord to end the scherzo, then nothing does. But by his use of bitonality of keys-a-third-apart Brian has forged his own new musical language from pre-existing forms; after this, nothing can be the same in his music. Nor was it.

Brian's use of bitonality here has the major alongside its relative minor. In the first movement, we noted that the concluding D major was not achieved by way of traditional harmony, through its dominant, A, but through the seventh, C sharp. The dislocation, and eventual engulfing, of D minor in the Scherzo came about through almost precisely the same process. The 'veritable storm' unleashed by the pinning of the minor mode to D by way of F echoes, at some considerable removes, the slide downwards by a

A Redeemed Artist

semitone to C sharp. As D flat in the first movement, this unfolded an "almost too beautiful" vista but as C sharp, also in the first movement but more importantly in the Scherzo, it becomes the drive by which D minor is finally removed. How this is related to the classical tonal principles which Brian has not utilised is remarkably subtle and inherently organic. The disestablishment of D minor came about initially through the long-term destabilising effect of the added sixth. The added sixth in C sharp minor is A – the very note which, in a classical cadence, would form the root of the penultimate chord, or key. The "veritable storm" is, as we have noted, in C sharp minor – the complete obverse of its enharmonic "too beautiful" equivalent, D flat major. But this storm is, in turn, rendered harmonically unstable, for all its fixation with C sharp minor, by precisely the same process – the added sixth, A. Once again, with D major established (but it could never be perceived as being precisely the same as that which ended the first movement), it is ultimately rendered unstable by the same process – its own added sixth, B. Not to play the added sixth B in the Scherzo's final D major chord further undermines Brian's unique processes. I am aware that Brian himself sanctioned the omission of this note from the chord in Boult's performance, but there are many instances in musical history of composers being persuaded to alter their earlier music. The original music of the 'Gothic' does not change, even if, more than forty years after it was written, the composer's own perception of it may have. Brian's original harmonic thoughts and processes are undoubtedly more organic and logical although the views of others must be respected. Nevertheless, the total absence of the 'classical' dominant preparation for D major throughout the first three movements of the 'Gothic' is further, and to my mind overwhelmingly conclusive, evidence of the tonal framework being cast in anything but traditional notions of sonata key relationships; the analysis of these movements in traditional terms may have some mnemonic usefulness, even if the music itself, at almost every turn, has contradicted such processes.

In his essay on the Symphony, Harold Truscott writes of Brian's setting of the Latin text seeming almost deliberately to destroy the meaning of the words by making them unintelligible, even to those familiar with the Latin text, and comparing Brian's seemingly deliberate obfuscation with the clarity of Berlioz's and Bruckner's settings. Yet Berlioz and Bruckner were both Catholics, and both would have assumed that virtually all members of their audiences would know the Latin text of the Te Deum well. Even in their settings there are passages where the words cannot always be made out.

On hearing an opera for the first time, in whatever language, most people, if they have the chance, will read a synopsis of the story, may even read the libretto if they have access to one, and in other ways prepare themselves for what they are about to see, with the result that their appreciation and understanding of the work is enhanced. Whilst we may bemoan the secularisation of present-day society – the Mass-media, as we noted earlier, having supplanted the Mass – it is not unreasonable to assume that members of audiences today would similarly prepare for a concert performance of a setting of any text by reading it beforehand, or by glancing at it during the performance, or by following the text if they were listening to a recording from the booklet provided.

Brian's religious beliefs, if he had any, were entirely his own affair. It is surely stretching the point too far to claim that, by

A Redeemed Artist

making it difficult to hear the words of the Te Deum clearly, Brian was showing his own lack of faith, and for him, the irrelevance of the text. A number of pious composers have set religious texts without ensuring that every word could be made out, and an equal number of irreligious composers have composed fine settings of sacred writings. The point, surely, is that considered purely as literature the Te Deum, the Hymn of St Ambrose, is a great Latin text. Brian undoubtedly had a mystical side to his character and it is perfectly understandable that he would be inspired by the Te Deum, and want to set the great words with great music from an artistic conviction and not from a religious one.

Brian's inspiration in Part II of the 'Gothic' barely falters; it is chock full of the most original and coherent ideas, all welded to the great tonal journey towards E major. Some listeners have been thrown by Brian's use of choral vocalising – the "la-la's" – but these fulfil several functions: the first is the instrumental lightening of tension through the clarinets' long march is echoed vocally at this point, a 'loosening-up' for a while as the summit of the work comes into view. The vocalising provides some relief to the choirs and to the listener; also, as the 'Gothic' is not just a setting of the Te Deum, but a vast symphonic panorama, the 'change' here from words to vocalisation is a further example of Brian's characteristic of the juxtaposition of opposites. As such, this is entirely indicative of his methods, for in addition the music surrounding this long but genuinely scherzando-like section (in character) sets it in sharp relief.

The published analyses of Part II of the 'Gothic' referred to on Page 91 are, in my view, wholly exceptional in their insight and sympathy, and readers keen to pursue their grasp of this work should study these writings, as well as Robert Simpson's and Deryck Cooke's programme notes for the 1961 and 1966 performances.

Brian surely knew full well what he had accomplished in the 'Gothic'. Having freed himself from the dual tyrannies of classical tonality on the one hand and Romantic self-projection on the other, and possessing a technical mastery which was quite the equal of that of any other living composer, Brian was able to pursue his artistic character as his muse, controlled by his creative intelligence, led him.

For years, as we know, he wrote large-scale work after large-scale work until, in the late 1950s, his later symphonies began to get the occasional hearing. Public and critics were thereby confronted with nothing less than music which did not behave in accordance with any known principles: Brian's language – although perfectly natural for him – was so new that most people forgot Schoenberg's principle: "A Chinese philosopher speaks Chinese; the important thing is, what does he say?" Because, to some ears, Brian's originality – in his orchestration and in his uniquely developed tonal structures – was unlike that of any other composer, he was patronisingly regarded as an amateur, made more plausible by the knowledge that he had rarely heard his own music; if he had, so the argument went, he would not have made the 'mistakes' that critics knew would be necessary to correct in order to make his music more 'acceptable'. The problem with such an argument is that Brian had heard quite a few of his own works, he had a radio, he had a large library of music and for many years was a music critic who heard live concerts daily. His knowledge of music was very great. He knew precisely what he was doing, as the logic of his music conclusively

A Redeemed Artist

demonstrates.

Brian's is modern music, technically: not the last throes of an 'outdated' self-regarding, gesturing Romanticism. His is music by a creative character so strong, so original that, given a listener willing to take the mere risk of giving his attention to this composer, he finds himself carried along on a journey to where he has never been before.

These journeys are not for the faint-hearted: but then, neither were those embarked upon in the music of Beethoven, Berlioz, Liszt or Wagner, or (most of) Richard Strauss, or (the whole of) Schoenberg, for that matter. As with these earlier masters, few listeners remain indifferent to Brian's music: nor is it a question of 'liking' it. Almost without exception, those commentators who airily dismissed his work made no genuine attempt to come to terms with it, to accept the challenges to the listener that his music poses. In the early 1950s, when I first began to study music, the symphonies of Bruckner, Elgar, Mahler, Rachmaninoff and Schoenberg – taking five great masters at random – were hardly ever heard in England. If a concert organisation so forgot itself as to programme one of their symphonies, it was soon brought into line by a hostile critical climate; no musician wanted to play music that the critics said was worthless, and the public, thus meekly taking their cue from the press, did not attend concerts which they would have been told the next day – assuming the newspapers' sub-editors had bothered to send anyone along – had been a waste of time.

Yet today we know – as the critics, concert-going public, record companies and broadcasting organisations of the 1950s apparently did not know in sufficient numbers – that the symphonies of those very different but equally great composers are imperishable masterpieces to which the public, given the chance, will respond. The role of the long-playing record in the general acceptance of these composers' symphonies was very important, and it was the newer companies that led the way: Vox, Nixa, Concert Artist, Delta and others. It is a relatively new company today, which, in its comparatively brief existence, has made a most important contribution worldwide to the expansion of recorded repertoire – Marco Polo – that will issue all of Brian's symphonies on compact disc; it is an opportunity that the public must, and will, take.

The enterprise of the Marco Polo company, as that of its predecessors in the late 1940s and early 1950s similarly showed, will afford music-lovers throughout the world the opportunity to study Brian's symphonic output at their own pace, an opportunity that the public has already, on the basis of sales of Marco Polo's initial releases in this series, shown itself more than ready to take. Although there are aspects of this company's recording of the 'Gothic' Symphony – particularly the tempo of the first movement – with which I disagree, the fact that such a pioneer recording of this legendary work stayed high in the American 'Billboard' classical best-selling charts month after month was highly encouraging. It is additionally encouraging that a man recently appointed to work for the Marco Polo company is my sympathetic colleague from CBS, Paul Myers; Brian's music could hardly be in more experienced hands.

Havergal Brian's music demands concentration, because it is, itself, highly concentrated; but it repays it a thousandfold to unprejudiced and attentive listeners who may have been initially attracted by the unusual facts of his composing life. They will find within his art, if their sensibilities lead them to persevere at their own speed, a body of great music unlike that of any other composer. Such is our redemption of Havergal Brian's lifetime of striving. It has been worth it.

Appendix I

The Havergal Brian Society

This book has been published to coincide with the 21st anniversary celebrations in 1995 of the founding of The Havergal Brian Society of Great Britain, an organisation formed to further interest in the work of the composer.

The Havergal Brian Society was created on an informal basis by Martin Grossel and James Reid Baxter in 1974, and by 1977 the structure of the Society was placed on a formal footing. The Society's inaugural General Meeting was held in January of that year and the Constitution of the Society was ratified at the January, 1978 Annual General Meeting. The Havergal Brian Society became a registered charity in June, 1978.

David J. Brown, who had taken the office of acting Secretary of the Society since June, 1976, then continued to serve as Secretary for many years. He edited the Society's first major publication, *Havergal Brian's Gothic Symphony: two studies* by Harold Truscott and Paul Rapoport, which also includes Havergal Brian's long-out-of-print essay, *How the 'Gothic' Symphony came to be written*, as a supplement. This important publication was issued in 1978, and is invaluable for those wishing to pursue their interest in this work in particular, and the composer in general. Copies of this book (87pp, softbound, with over 130 music examples and five illustrations) can be obtained from the Society, priced £10.00, post free.

The Society has also published Havergal Brian's complete

Appendix I

piano works and has assisted in the subvention of commercial recordings of the composer's music. In addition, the Society issues regular newsletters.

The aims of The Havergal Brian Society are to further public knowledge of Brian's compositions by supporting and sponsoring their publication, performance and recording. Details of the Society's activities can be obtained from:

> Dr Alan Marshall,
> Administrative Secretary,
> 5 Eastbury Road,
> Watford,
> Herts WD1 4PT,
> England.

Appendix II

Performances of the 'Gothic' Symphony

June 24th, 1961. Central Hall, Westminster, London
London Philharmonic Choir (chorusmaster: Frederick Jackson);
Kingsway Choral Society (chorusmaster: Donald Cashmore);
London Orpheus Choir (chorusmaster: James Gaddarn);
Hendon Grammar School Choir (Director of Music: Charles
Western); Royal Military School of Music (Offstage Fanfare
conducted by Student Bandmaster D. Stannard);
Alan Harverson, organ
Noelle Barker, soprano; Jean Evans, contralto; Kenneth Bowen,
tenor; John Shirley-Quirk, bass
Polyphonia Symphony Orchestra (leader: Robert Cooper)
Bryan Fairfax, conductor

October 30th, 1966. Royal Albert Hall, London
BBC Chorus; BBC Choral Society; City of London Choir
(conductor: Donald Cashmore); Hampstead Choral Society
(conductor: Martindale Sidwell); Choir of Emanuel School
(conductor: Christian Strover); Orpington Junior Singers
(conductor: Sheila Mossman)
Honor Sheppard, soprano; Shirley Minty, contralto; Ronald
Dowd, tenor; Roger Stalman, bass
BBC Symphony Orchestra (leader: Hugh Maguire)
Sir Adrian Boult, conductor

Appendix II

May 21st 1978. Victoria Hall, Hanley, Stoke-on-Trent, Staffordshire
Keele Chamber Choir; Margaret Wharam Choir, Solihull; Nantwich and District Choral Society; Oriana Choir, Macclesfield; Potteries Choral Society; Stone Choral Society; Ashbourne Parish Church Boys' Choir; Goudhurst College Girls' Choir; Nantwich Parish Church Boys' Choir; Prestbury Boys' Choir; Prestbury Girls' Choir
Marjorie Tapley, soprano; Jean Reavley, contralto; Eric Baskeyfield, tenor; Philip Ravenscroft, bass
The Stoke Gothic Symphony Orchestra
Trevor Stokes, conductor

May 25th, 1980. Royal Albert Hall, London
BBC Singers (trained by Ronald Corp); London Symphony Chorus (directed by Richard Hickox); London Philharmonic Choir (trained by Malcolm Hicks); BBC Club Choir (conductor: Ronald Corp); Hampstead Choral Society (conductor: Martindale Sidwell); Members of the Bach Choir, English Chamber Choir (director: Guy Protheroe); Members of BBC Symphony Chorus, the Royal Choral Society and the Goldsmiths' Choral Union (all trained by Brian Wright); Orpheus Girls' Choir (conductor: John Railton); Colfe's School Choir (conductor: Colin Howard)
Jane Manning, soprano; Shirley Minty, contralto; John Mitchinson, tenor; David Thomas, bass
London Symphony Orchestra (leader: Irving Arditti)
Ole Schmidt, conductor.

October 10th, 1976. Royal Albert Hall, London
Movements 1-3 only.
New Philharmonia Orchestra (leader: Desmond Bradley)
Sir Charles Groves, conductor.

Appendix III

Released recordings
of the 'Gothic' Symphony

1. Aries LP 2601 (2xLP)
Honor Sheppard, soprano; Shirley Minty, contralto; Ronald Dowd, tenor; Roger Stalman, bass
BBC Chorus, BBC Choral Society, City of London Choir, Hampstead Choral Society, Choir of Emanuel School, Orpington Junior Singers
BBC Symphony Orchestra
Sir Adrian Boult, conductor
Unauthorised 'pirate' release from the BBC broadcast of the performance on October 30th, 1966

2. Marco Polo 8.223280-281 (2xCD)
Eva Jenisova, soprano; Dagmar Peckova, contralto; Vladimir Dolezal, tenor; Peter Mikulas, bass
Slovak Philharmonic Choir, Slovak Opera Chorus, Slovak Folk Ensemble Chorus, Lucnica Chorus, Bratislava City Choir, Bratislava Children's Choir, Youth Echo Choir (Pavol Prochazka, chorusmaster)
CSR Symphony Orchestra, Bratislava; Slovak Philharmonic Orchestra
Ondrej Lenard, conductor

HAVERGAL BRIAN

Recorded at the Concert Hall of Czechoslovak Radio Bratislava, March 29th-31st, October 16th-22nd, 1989.
Producer: Gunter Appenheimer. Musical Adviser: David J. Brown.
This recording was not made concurrently with a public performance.

INDEX

Abba 80
Adler, F. Charles 38
Altarus Record Company 10
Appenheimer, Gunter 118
Arditti, Irving 115
Aries Records 104, 117
Arnell, Richard 58, 80
Arnold, Sir Malcolm 46
Ashborne Parish Church Boys'
    Choir 115
Asher, M. Richard 65
Augener & Co Ltd 19, 62

Bach Choir 115
Baddeley, Mary 29
Balsam, Artur 24
Barker, Noelle 114
Barsham, Eve 28
Bartók, Bela 94-5
Baskeyfield, Eric 115
Bate, Stanley 58
Baxter, James Reid 112
BBC Choral Society 114, 117
BBC Chorus 114, 117
BBC Club Choir 115
BBC Singers 115
BBC Symphony Chorus 115

BBC Symphony Orchestra 28-30,
    59, 114, 117
Beard, Paul 28-9
Beecham, Sir Thomas 28, 50, 58-9,
    80
Beethoven, Ludwig van 31, 60, 69,
    75, 89, 93-6, 103, 109
Benjamin, Arthur 86
Berg, Alban 71
Berlioz, Hector 69, 93-5, 106, 109
Berners, Lord 80
Bernstein, Leonard 63, 65-6, 77-8,
    89
Bizet, Georges 78
Bliss, Sir Arthur 86
Blond, Anthony, Ltd 21
Boosey & Hawkes Ltd 46
Boulez, Pierre 60, 62, 78
Boult, Sir Adrian 13-14, 29, 58-63,
    70, 73, 83, 87, 104-5, 114, 117
Bowen, Kenneth 114
Bowen, York 58
Bradley, Desmond 116
Brahms, Johannes 8, 94
Bratislava Children's Choir 117
Bratislava City Choir 117
Breunig, Christopher 10

119

HAVERGAL BRIAN

'Brian, Bill' 51
Havergal Brian Society 7, 12, 91, 112-13
Brian, Havergal: *Works*
  Agamemnon 42
  Cello Concerto 74
  Cello Concerto No 2 (projected) 63
  Comedy Overture (The Jolly Miller) 56, 74
  Concerto for Orchestra 74
  Dr Merryheart Overture 15, 18, 30
  Double Fugue in E flat 15, 19
  English Suite No 1 - 67
  English Suite No 5 - 80, 81, 85
  Fantastic Symphony (originally No 1) 36, 59, 71
  Fantastic Variations on an Old Rhyme 18, 63
  Festal Dance 59
  Festival Fanfare 84, 86
  For Valour 67
  Hero and Leander 67
  Prelude and Fugue in C minor 15-16, 19
  Prometheus Unbound 72
  Psalm 23 - 67, 78, 80-81, 85, 96-7
  Psalm 137 - 67
  String Quartets (projected) 63
  Symphonies: new numbering
  Symphony No 1 'Gothic' 10, 18, 25-7, 34, 36, 38-9, 45-8, 50-51, 53-4, 57-63, 65, 68-72,

Symphony No 1 'Gothic' (*continued*) 74, 77-8, 83-4, 87, 91-2, 97-108, 110, 114-17
Symphony No 2 - 71-2
Symphony No 3 - 71, 75-6
Symphony No 4 'Das Siegeslied' 62, 71-2
Symphony No 5 'Wine of Summer' 71-2
Symphony No 6 'Sinfonia Tragica' 37, 72, 77
Symphony No 7 - 72
Symphony No 8 - 14, 20, 22, 28-30, 43, 72-4
Symphony No 9 - 15, 20-23, 27-8, 30, 55-6, 72-4
Symphony No 10 - 24, 27-30, *52*, 72-5, 77, 79, 102
Symphony No 11 - 30-31, 45, 73-4
Symphony No 12 - 30-31, 58, 73-4
Symphony No 13 - 34-5, 55
Symphony No 14 - 35-6, 55, 72, 74
Symphony No 15 - 37, 56
Symphony No 16 - 7-9, 11-12, 40-41, 55, 77
Symphony No 17 - 55
Symphony No 18 - 54-57, 72, 74-75
Symphony No 19 - 55
Symphony No 20 - 56
Symphony No 21 - 72-4, 77, 79

Index

Brian Havergal: *Works (continued)*
    Symphony No 22 'Symphonia Brevis' 72, 74, 80-81, 85
    Symphony No 27 - 59-60
    Symphony No 29 - 63
    The Tigers 12, 68
    Violin Concerto (No 2) 72
Brighton Festival Chorus 85
British National Opera Company 48
British National Party 46
Britten, Lord Benjamin 17, 21, 38, 53
Brown, David J. 112, 118
Bruckner, Anton 11, 17-18, 38, 50, 92, 94, 102-3, 106, 109
Burford, Ray 30, 65, 82
Busoni, Ferruccio 51
Byrd, William 70

Cardus, Sir Neville 50
Cashmore, Donald 114
Casson, Sir Hugh 23
CBS Records 65-6, 78, 80-82, 85, 110
Chandos Records 86
Chester, J.W., & Co 62
Chopin, Frédéric 96, 98
Cincinnati Symphony Orchestra 25
City of London Choir 114, 117
Cockshott, Gerald 49
Colfe's School Choir 115
Concert Artist Record Company 110

Cooke, Deryck 60-61, 87, 108
Cooper, Geoffrey Lee 9-10, 24, 39
Cooper, Robert 114
Copland, Aaron 95
Corp, Ronald 115
Couzens, Brian 86
Crankshaw, Geoffrey 8-9
Cranz & Co Ltd 26-7, 44
Crosse, Gordon 58
Czech Radio Symphony Orchestra 117

Davidson, Duane 37
Debussy, Claude Achille 95
Del Mar, Norman 30, 58, 63
Delta Record Company 110
Deutsche Grammophon [DGG] 78
Dolezal, Vladimir 117
Doran, Mark 7, 9, 10
Douglas, Lord Alfred 71
Dorward, David 37, 46
Dowd, Ronald 114, 117
Dussek, Jan 96
Dvořák, Antonin 94

Et Cetera Records 80
Elgar, Sir Edward 24-5, 84, 86, 88, 109
Elizabeth II, Queen 84
Eltham Music Club 13-14, 24, 30, 34, 46, 65
Emanuel School Choir 114, 117
English Chamber Choir 115

121

English National Opera Orchestra 84

Evans, Jean 114

Fairfax, Bryan 37-9, 46-48, 51, 54-6, 60-61, 114
Farah, Empress of Iran 83
Foreman, Lewis 81
Fredman, Myer 8
Fuller, Jim 61-3
Fuller, Yvonne 62
Furnivall, Mrs Jean 10

Gaddarn, James 114
Galway, James 82
Gardner, John 63
Gerhardt, Charles 83
Glass, Douglas 43, 46
Glock, Sir William 57-9
Goethe, Johann Wolfgang von 87
Golder, A.K. 46
Golder, Madeline 46
Goldsmiths' Choral Union 115
Goossens I, Eugène 26, 48
Goossens II, Eugène 26, 48
Goossens, Sir Eugène 10, 24-7, 46-50, 59, 61, 101
Goudhurst College Girls' Choir 115
Greenfield, Edward 61
Grossel, Martin 112
Groves, Sir Charles 116

Hampstead Choral Society 114, 115, 117

Harty, Sir Hamilton 59, 61
Harverson, Alan 114
Hatton, Graham 44
Head, Leslie 71
Heltay, Laszlo 78, 80-81, 85
Hendon Grammar School Choir 114
Henze, Hans Werner 24-5
Hickox, Richard 115
Hicks, Malcolm 115
Hindemith, Paul 95
Hitler, Adolf 26
Hoddinott, Alun 37
Holst, Gustav 100
Howard, Colin 115
Howard, Leslie 98

Jackson, Frederick 114
Jacob, Gordon 86
Jacobs, Peter 10
Jenisova, Eva 117
Johnson, Edward 10, 78
Johnson, W.W. 46

Kasket, Madeleine 82
Keeffe, Bernard 59
Keele Chamber Choir 115
Kelleher, James 7-8, 11-12
Keller, Hans 1
Kensington Symphony Orchestra 71
Kingsway Choral Society 114
Korngold, Erich Wolfgang 83
Korngold, George 83

Index

Lake, Leslie 84
Laming, Peter 13, 24
Lea-Jones, Nigel 10
Leavins, Arthur 28-30
Lehmann, Lotte 62
Leicestershire Schools Symphony
    Orchestra 77, 79, 82, 85
Lenard, Ondrej 117
Lengnick, Alfred, & Co Ltd 14,
    43-4
Leningrad Philharmonic Orchestra
    83
Levi, Philip 51
Liszt, Ferenc 93-4, 109
Lloyd, George 42
Locke Brass Consort 86
London Orchestra of St Cecilia 7
London Orpheus Choir 114
London Philharmonic Choir 114,
    115
London Philharmonic Orchestra
    8, 14
London Symphony Chorus 115
London Symphony Orchestra 30,
    115
Loughran, James 77
Lucnica Chorus 117
Lyrita Recorded Edition 77

MacDonald, Malcolm 10, 31,
    40-41, 44, 63, 91-2, 98, 104, 108
McKenzie, Angus 66, 77, 81, 85
Maguire, Hugh 114
Mahler, Gustav 11, 17-18, 31, 37-8,
    50, 63, 65, 70, 92-3, 109

Main, Pamela 10
Manning, Jane 115
Marco Polo Record Company
    110-111, 117
Margaret Wharam Choir, Solihull
    115
Marshall, Alan 10, 113
Martelli, Carlo 58
Mason, Colin 61
Mather, Don 24, 46
Mendelssohn, Felix 96
Mikulas, Peter 117
Milhaud, Darius 65, 95
Minneapolis Symphony Orchestra
    38
Minty, Shirley 114, 115, 117
Mitchinson, John 115
Mitropoulos, Dmitri 38
Moody Manners Opera Company
    48
Mossman, Sheila 114
Mott the Hoople 80
Mozart, Wolfgang Amadeus 24
Musica Viva 44
Mussorgsky, Modest 68
Myers, Paul 66, 77, 110

Nantwich and District Choral
    Society 115
Nantwich Parish Church Boys'
    Choir 115
National Federation of Gramo-
    phone Societies 13, 46
Nettel, Reginald 15, 17
New Philharmonia Orchestra 116

Newman, Bill 65
Newmarch, Rosa 59
Newstone, Harry 30
Nielsen, Carl 11, 94, 97
Nixa Record Company 110

Oberstein, Maurice L. 65
Oord, Gerry 83
Orga, Ateş 83
Oriana Choir, Macclesfield 115
Orpheus Girls' Choir 115
Orpington Junior Singers 114, 117
Osostowicz, Krysia 8
Ottoway, Hugh 14, 22

Payne, Derek 13
Pears, Sir Peter 21
Peckova, Dagmar 117
Philharmonia Orchestra 27, 30, 73
Philips Records 24
Pinkett, Eric 77, 80-1, 85
Polyphonia Symphony Orchestra 37-8, 51, 114
Pope, Stanley 24, 27, 29-30, 63, 73
Potteries Choral Society 115
Prelude Records 40
Prenn, Oliver 21
Prestbury Boys' Choir 115
Prestbury Girls' Choir 115
Prochazka, Pavol 117
Protheroe, Guy 115
Pudney, Douglas 24

Queen's Hall Orchestra 59

Rachmaninoff, Serge 11, 109
Railton, John 115
Ramsey, Basil 40
Rapoport, Paul 91, 112
Ravel, Maurice 48
Ravenscroft, Philip 115
Rawsthorne, Alan 17-8
RCA Records 40, 82-3, 86
Reavley, Jean 115
Reger, Max 19
Richards, Denby 10
Rimsky-Korsakov, Nikolai 68
Robson, William 80, 85
Rosa Opera Company, Carl 48
Rossiter, David 80
Roussel, Albert 48
Royal Academy of Music 7
Royal Choral Society 115
Royal Military School of Music 114
Royal Philharmonic Orchestra 24, 28
Rubbra, Edmund 14, 21, 84, 86

St Pancras Arts Festival 51
Schmidt, Ole 115
Schoenberg, Arnold 71, 95, 108-9
Schott & Co Ltd 43-4
Schubert, Franz 18-19, 70
Schumann, Robert 17, 24, 93
Schwarz, Rudolf 28-30
Shah of Iran 83
Shelley, Percy Bysshe 72
Sheppard, Honor 114, 117
Shirley-Quirk, John 114

Index

Shostakovich, Dmitri 41
Sibelius, Jean 31, 94
Sidwell, Martindale 114-15
Simpson, Robert 9-10, 13-15,
    20-24, 28, 30-31, 34, 36-8,
    41, 43-6, 54-5, 57-61, 63,
    74, 77, 81, 84-7, 97, 108
Slobodskaya, Oda 62
Slovak Folk Ensemble Chorus 117
Slovak Opera Chorus 117
Slovak Philharmonic Choir 117
Slovak Philharmonic Orchestra
    117
Smith, Malcolm 10
Stalman, Roger 114, 117
Stannard, Student Bandmaster D.
    114
Stobart, James 84, 86
Stockhausen, Karlheinz 75
Stoke Gothic Symphony Orches-
    tra 115
Stokes, Trevor 115
Stone Choral Society 115
Stone, F. Felgate 50-51
Strauss, Richard 42, 59, 61, 70, 93,
    109
Stravinsky, Igor 77, 95
Strover, Christian 114
Szaybo, Roslav 81

Tapley, Marjorie 115
Taylor, Paul 85
Tchaikovsky, Peter Ilych 93
Thomas, David 115

Thorne, Mike 66, 77, 81
The Three Degrees 80
Tippett, Sir Michael 63, 66, 86
Tjeknavorian, Loris 82-3
Tovey, Sir Donald Francis 59, 61,
    70
Truscott, Harold 9-10, 16-20, 28,
    61, 90-93, 98, 101, 103, 106,
    112

Unicorn Records 77, 79, 82
United Music Publishers 44

Vaughan Williams, Ralph 17, 80,
    95
Verdi, Giuseppe 42, 80
Victoria, Queen 96
Vivaldi, Antonio 11
Vox Record Company 110

Wagner, Richard 59, 92-94, 109
Walker, Robert 40
Walter, Bruno 37
Walton, Sir William 17-8, 86
Warr, Eric 55
Western, Charles 114
Wilkinson, Kenneth 83
Williams, John 78
Wind Music Society 37
Wood, Sir Henry 59, 61
Wright, Brian 115

Youth Echo Choir 117

Other music titles by
Robert Matthew-Walker
published by DGR Books:

Edvard Grieg: A biographical study

This is the first original biography in English of the Norwegian master to be published for over twenty years. It includes new material relating to Grieg's ancestry and to his music which has never before been published, together with extensive quotations from Grieg's own writings, specially translated for this book.

"A penetrating account of the life and times of Edvard Grieg, this book admirably identifies his place among world composers and at the same time chronicles every stage in the development of the special characteristics that made him Norway's National Hero both during his lifetime and since his death.

It should appeal to both the musician and the music-lover. To someone who still thinks of Grieg as a miniaturist who also wrote a piano concerto this book will be a revelation."

Sir Alexander Gibson

"This fine study shows new insight into Grieg's mastery of both larger and smaller forms, and makes us aware of Grieg's little appreciated influence on later masters."

Dr. Alun Francis

ISBN 1 898343 00 4   Hardback, £12.95

THE RECORDINGS OF EDVARD GRIEG:
A Tradition Captured

From 1897 until 1905 the Norwegian composer Edvard Grieg made thirty-five recordings, principally of his own music, on private cylinders, on commercial discs for the Gramophone Company, and on piano-rolls for three different companies – Aeolian, Hupfeld and Welte-Mignon. This vitally important recorded legacy has remained virtually unknown, even to Grieg specialists. The author has traced the fascinating story of the early years of recording in all three systems, and how Edvard Grieg – then in his fifties and sixties – became the first great composer to make commercial recordings. This story is here told for the first time, with extracts from Grieg's diaries and from reminiscences by his contemporaries.

"The opening chapter dealing with the significance of historic recordings is particularly good. . . there are full details of the recordings themselves together with an important listing of archive recordings of Grieg's music by artists who knew the composer personally . . ."

Malcolm Walker, *Gramophone*

Illustrated

ISBN 1 898343 02 0   Softback £6.95

Finalist in the Association for Recorded Sound Collections International Awards, New York, 1994

ALUN HODDINOTT ON RECORD:
A Composer and the Gramophone

Foreword by Sir Charles Groves

This book, the first of its kind, relates the enthralling story of how a living composer's commercial discography developed from small beginnings to the point where, with over seventy works recorded, Alun Hoddinott had a major new cello concerto recorded by Rostropovich and a work in the pop album charts in the same month.

"I can confirm that this is not merely a well-researched compendium of facts and numbers but also a very good read . . . the introductory half-dozen chapters, outlining the composer's growth and development linked with the record business and the outstanding help from the Welsh Arts Council, are written with such ease of communication that I defy anybody who has never heard of Hoddinott to read them without rushing out to the nearest record shop. This is a delightful book which is invaluable for music-lovers, record-collectors, students, librarians, and followers of contemporary music."
Denby Richards, Editor, *Musical Opinion*

ISBN 1 898343 01 2   Softback £5.95

Published by:
DGR Books,
Kenwyn, Greensplat, St. Austell, Cornwall PL26 8XX, England.